Stanford 9* Workbook

Grade 3

* Stanford Achievement Test, Ninth Edition ©. The Stanford 9 is a product of Harcourt Brace Educational Measurement, which is not affiliated with this book.

By the Staff of Kaplan, Inc.

Simon & Schuster

NEW YORK · LONDON · SINGAPORE · SYDNEY · TORONTO

Kaplan Publishing

Published by Simon & Schuster
1230 Avenue of the Americas
New York, NY 10020

For bulk sales to schools, colleges, and universities, please contact: Order Department, Simon & Schuster, 100 Front Street, Riverside, NJ 08075. Phone: 800-223-2336, Fax: 800-943-9831.

Project Editor: Larissa Shmailo
Contributing Editor: Marc Bernstein, Marcy Bullmaster, and Phillip Vlahakis.
Page Layout: Laurel Douglas
Art and Design: Denise Hoff, Pamela Beaulieu, Alissa Caratozzolo, Laurel Douglas, Erika Quinoz-Heineman, Jobim Rose
Cover Design: Cheung Tai
Production Editor: Maude Spekes
Editorial Coordinator: Déa Alessandro
Production Manager: Michael Shevlin
Executive Editor: Del Franz

Manufactured in the United States of America

Published simultaneously in Canada

Special thanks: Drew Johnson, Rudy Robles

October 2001

10 9 8 7 6 5 4 3 2

ISBN 0-7432-2787-5

All of the practice questions in this book were created by the authors to illustrate question types. They are not actual test questions. For more information about the Stanford 9, visit the Harcourt Brace Educational Measurement website at www.hemweb.com.

CONTENTS

A Special Note to Parents

Standardized tests . . . the thought conjures up images of impersonal classrooms, No. 2 pencils, and the fast-moving hands of a looming black clock. It doesn't sound like a lot of fun. And your child will be taking a lot of them, including, in more and more school districts, the Stanford 9.

However you may feel about them, standardized tests are part of school life today. And pending legislation in Congress will soon require even more testing in elementary school grades. Your child's teachers can help your child learn much of the material covered on these tests. However, in many states, teachers do not teach test-taking skills for standardized tests, nor do most schools give practice tests to prepare children for the actual test. It's also not certain that everything on the test will be covered in your child's school curriculum. So your child can especially benefit from your thoughtful participation in the test-taking process to succeed on the Stanford 9.

WHAT IS THE STANFORD 9?

The Stanford 9, or the Stanford Achievement Test, Ninth Edition, is a widely used set of tests published and developed by Harcourt Brace Educational Measurement. The Stanford 9 consists of multiple-choice tests in Mathematics—Problem Solving; Mathematics—Procedures; Reading Vocabulary; Reading Comprehension; Language; and Spelling; there are also open-ended assessments in reading, mathematics, and study skills. States and school districts tailor the test to their own requirements by using all the test sections or by picking various components ("mix and matching"). At press time, the Stanford 9 is being used in Alabama, Arkansas, Arizona, California, the District of Columbia, Georgia, Florida, Hawaii, South Dakota, Utah, West Virginia, and Virginia; other states may also implement the test in their school districts in the near future.

In test language, the Stanford 9 is called a "norm-referenced test," which means it is designed to compare your child's performance to that of other children in a national sample. The test measures a student's knowledge in broad content areas, rather than of the particular curriculum taught in his or her school. The student's scores are given by percentiles. These rank students with others in the nation at the same grade level who took the test. If a student scored 78 in total reading, for example, it means that 77 percent of the other students who are in the same grade who took this test scored lower. Conversely, 21 percent scored higher.

In addition, performance standards based on the judgments of teachers are used in some localities; these provide information about what the third-grader should know and be able to do according to standards accepted by the school, school district, or school board. Four levels of performance standards are available for the Stanford 9:

Level 4 – *Advanced*, signifies superior performance beyond grade level mastery.

Level 3 – *Proficient*, represents solid academic performance, indicating that students are prepared for the next grade.

Level 2 – *Basic*, denotes partial mastery of the knowledge and skills that are fundamental for satisfactory work.

Level 1 – *Below Basic*, indicates less than partial mastery of a subject area

IS THE STANFORD 9 TEST IMPORTANT?

Today, with national legislation for mandatory testing for grades 3–8 pending, tests like the Stanford 9 are more important than ever and have greater consequences. In many states, performance on the Stanford 9 test already has a significant impact on both the student and the school district. Based on test performance, some states rank all schools, showing how well or how poorly their students fared on the exam. Schools that do badly may face the possibility of having superintendents, principals, or teachers fired based on their low performance.

As for the individual third-grader, some school districts are proposing that students who fail the Stanford 9 tests not be promoted to the next grade. The Stanford 9 tests are not necessarily the sole factor in promotion/retention decisions, however. Other factors, such as attendance, teacher recommendation, and performance on local assessment tests may also be used by the local district to decide whether or not a student can advance to the next grade level.

HOW CAN I HELP?

By buying this workbook, you've already shown your concern about and involvement in your child's education. Tests are stressful, and standardized tests can cause a great deal of anxiety for children, especially if they are unfamiliar with them. Familiarity with test conditions, practice, and basic test-taking skills can help reduce test anxiety, increase your child's confidence, and lead to higher scores.

The practice tests in this workbook are designed to test important concepts in math and language. They are not sample Stanford 9 tests, but will provide your child with experience taking multiple-choice tests under timed conditions, and with using a variety of test-taking strategies for different kinds of questions. They can also help identify areas of weakness in subject areas.

To start, you and your child can read the **Introduction** to this book, especially the "How to Use This Book" section, together. Then have your child take the first test under timed conditions. Your child does not have to finish all the sections in a row, but should not take any breaks while working on a section. Afterwards, review the **Answers and Explanations for Practice Test A**. Go over the scores and answers to identify any areas of weakness. You can then work on these subjects together.

Before your child takes the second test, read the **Test-Taking Strategies** chapter. Go over the tips and strategies for each section of the test, especially any section that seemed difficult the first time. When he or she is ready, your child can take the second test.

Standardized tests may not seem like a lot of fun, but with a little help from you, your child can approach them with confidence and succeed on test day.

Introduction

This workbook will help you get ready for the Grade 3 Stanford 9 test. The two tests in this book let you test yourself on important subjects in math and English. These exams will also give you practice answering multiple-choice questions and taking tests that are timed. These are not "sample" Stanford 9 tests. But the exams in this workbook will help you learn test-taking skills and find out what you know and what you don't know. That way, you can pay special attention to your weakest areas and be prepared to do well on the day of the real Stanford 9 test.

HOW TO USE THIS BOOK

This book contains two tests. Each covers subjects such as reading, math, language, and spelling. Take the first test (which starts on page 1), first. There is no need to study or prepare for this exam since the goal is to find out how well you can score without any preparation.

Mark your answers to the questions using a No. 2 pencil on the answer sheets at the end of each section. Time yourself when you take the test; limit yourself to the time listed at the start of each test section. You don't have to finish all the sections in a row, but do not stop working on any one section until your time is up. Taking breaks during a section is not the best way to get ready for the Stanford 9. There will be no breaks during a section during the real Stanford 9.

The tests you'll be taking are divided into the following sections:

Subject	Number of Questions	Time
Reading Vocabulary	30 questions	20 minutes
Reading Comprehension	54 questions	50 minutes
Mathematics—Problem Solving	46 questions	50 minutes
Mathematics—Procedures	30 questions	30 minutes
Language	48 questions	45 minutes
Spelling	30 questions	25 minutes

Remember that there is no guessing penalty on the Stanford 9 test—that means no points are subtracted for wrong answers. So answer all the questions even if you have to guess. Use process of elimination—crossing out the answers you know are wrong—to help you make better guesses.

It's also a good idea to write down all your work, especially for the math questions. Try to work at a steady pace, and don't get stuck on any one question. If you have time, you can always go back to look at it again.

Once you finish the first test, look at the explanations that begin on page 89. Your answers to the questions on the first test—especially the ones you answered incorrectly—will show you the subjects you need to work on. If you scored low in one area, call that a "Hot Spot." You should find extra help for that subject. Ask your teachers, parents, or friends for advice.

While working on your Hot Spots, take some time to look over the **Test-Taking Strategies** beginning on page 113. You may have already used some of these strategies on your own during the first test, but it's important you try to use them all on the second exam.

On the first test, you will answer questions without a special plan, but after studying the **Test-Taking Strategies** section, you'll take the next test with a clearer idea of how to answer each kind of question. Working on a question with the right strategy not only means you have a better chance of getting that question right, it also means you will be less nervous about the test. By learning all the strategies, you'll understand what you need to do to score well on the Stanford 9, and this will help you feel more confident.

Once you have worked on your Hot Spots and studied the various strategies, take the second exam (page 119). Make sure you time yourself on each section. Your score on the second test should be higher than your score on the first test because:

(1) You have studied more.

(2) You are comfortable with the look and feel of the test.

After you take and grade your second test, look for the subjects in which your score was low. Use your study time to work on those areas.

If your score on the second test falls or stays the same, don't worry. Remember, this is just practice and these tests don't count! A low score just means you have more work to do. Sometimes scores drop because you are trying out a new test-taking technique for the first time. You are doing the right thing by testing yourself and studying. Keep practicing and you will be ready for the Stanford 9 on test day!

Practice
Test A

Section 1: Reading Vocabulary

20 Minutes

30 Questions

Directions: *Make sure you have a watch to time yourself and a No. 2 pencil. When you are ready, start timing yourself, and spend 20 minutes answering the questions in this section. Mark your answers on the Answer Sheet at the end of this section. If you are finished before the time is up, check over your work.*

Reading Vocabulary

Synonyms

Directions

Pick the word or phrase that means the same, or nearly the same, as the underlined word. Then mark the correct space for the answer that you have picked.

Sample

To <u>conquer</u> is to —

- Ⓐ control
- ● defeat
- Ⓒ lose
- Ⓓ support

1 To <u>elect</u> someone means to —

- Ⓐ find them
- Ⓑ choose them
- Ⓒ catch them
- Ⓓ teach them

2 To be <u>certain</u> is to be —

- Ⓕ sure
- Ⓖ funny
- Ⓗ fast
- Ⓙ smart

3 To <u>applaud</u> is to —

- Ⓐ point
- Ⓑ chase
- Ⓒ bake
- Ⓓ clap

4 A <u>giggle</u> is a kind of —

- Ⓕ laugh
- Ⓖ book
- Ⓗ dessert
- Ⓙ music

5 If something is <u>private</u> it is —

- Ⓐ from a library
- Ⓑ your own
- Ⓒ on time
- Ⓓ for sale

KAPLAN

6 To <u>invent</u> is to —

Ⓔ rest
Ⓖ create
Ⓗ chase
Ⓘ write

7 To <u>defend</u> means to —

Ⓐ protect
Ⓑ lift
Ⓒ dent
Ⓓ notice

8 <u>Narrow</u> means —

Ⓔ open
Ⓖ tall
Ⓗ thin
Ⓘ scared

9 To <u>confess</u> is to —

Ⓐ admit
Ⓑ stay
Ⓒ buy
Ⓓ stain

10 A <u>setting</u> is a —

Ⓔ friend
Ⓖ place
Ⓗ task
Ⓘ game

11 Someone who is <u>absent</u> is —

Ⓐ not here
Ⓑ loud
Ⓒ surprised
Ⓓ very short

12 An <u>organization</u> is a kind of —

Ⓔ school
Ⓖ building
Ⓗ group
Ⓘ furniture

GO ON

13 To <u>sketch</u> something is to —

   Ⓐ act it
   Ⓑ read it
   Ⓒ draw it
   Ⓓ photograph it

14 <u>Swap</u> means to —

   Ⓕ light
   Ⓖ lead
   Ⓗ hide
   Ⓙ trade

15 A <u>stroll</u> is a kind of —

   Ⓐ hug
   Ⓑ walk
   Ⓒ joke
   Ⓓ song

16 To <u>chill</u> something is to —

   Ⓕ wear it
   Ⓖ throw it
   Ⓗ cool it
   Ⓙ want it

17 To <u>drift</u> means to —

   Ⓐ flow
   Ⓑ wander
   Ⓒ look
   Ⓓ stand

18 The <u>summit</u> of something is its —

   Ⓕ face
   Ⓖ top
   Ⓗ foot
   Ⓙ edge

GO ON

Multiple Meanings

Directions

Read the sentence in each of the boxes below. Then pick the answer that uses the underlined word in the same way as the sentence in the box. Mark the correct space for the answer that you have picked.

Sample

> He used the <u>light</u> from the stars to find his way through the woods.

In which sentence does the word <u>light</u> mean the same thing as in the sentence above?

- Ⓐ He was able to carry the <u>light</u> box of books up several flights of stairs.
- ● The <u>light</u> given off by the lamp was not enough to brighten the entire room.
- Ⓒ It can be dangerous for a <u>light</u> car to drive on mountain roads on a very windy day.
- Ⓓ The dentist's patients like him because he has a <u>light</u> touch with his instruments.

---

19 > We will <u>load</u> the car in the morning.

In which sentence does the word <u>load</u> mean the same thing as in the sentence above?

- Ⓐ That horse is carrying a full <u>load</u>.
- Ⓑ Runners try to <u>load</u> the bases.
- Ⓒ The moving company will <u>load</u> our furniture.
- Ⓓ I will put a <u>load</u> of dirty clothes into the wash.

20 > I want to live <u>by</u> the ocean when I grow up.

In which sentence does the word <u>by</u> mean the same thing as in the sentence above?

- Ⓕ She walked right <u>by</u> me without saying hello.
- Ⓖ The book was written <u>by</u> a good author.
- Ⓗ We won <u>by</u> many points.
- Ⓙ My house is <u>by</u> the school.

21 > It was an <u>honor</u> to be chosen.

In which sentence does the word <u>honor</u> mean the same thing as in the sentence above?

- Ⓐ I received an <u>honor</u> at the dinner.
- Ⓑ In <u>honor</u> of her birthday, we had a party.
- Ⓒ I try to <u>honor</u> my parents.
- Ⓓ He is a man of great <u>honor</u>.

GO ON

22 To play dodge ball, make a <u>ring</u> around the person in the middle.

In which sentence does the word <u>ring</u> mean the same thing as in the sentence above?

- Ⓕ The wet glass left a <u>ring</u> on the table.
- Ⓖ I answered the phone on the third <u>ring</u>.
- Ⓗ I will <u>ring</u> the doorbell first.
- Ⓙ The chorus stood in a <u>ring</u> around the conductor.

23 I want to <u>watch</u> television tonight.

In which sentence does the word <u>watch</u> mean the same thing as in the sentence above?

- Ⓐ Our dog is a very mean <u>watch</u> dog.
- Ⓑ Did you have good seats to <u>watch</u> the game?
- Ⓒ I want a new <u>watch</u> for my birthday.
- Ⓓ The guard was on night <u>watch</u>.

24 I can't wait to go <u>back</u> and visit my old town.

In which sentence does the word <u>back</u> mean the same thing as in the sentence above?

- Ⓕ Be careful not to hurt your <u>back</u> on the trampoline.
- Ⓖ My mom will <u>back</u> up the car so we can get in.
- Ⓗ Give me a call when you are <u>back</u> from school.
- Ⓙ I stood in the <u>back</u> of the line because I am so tall.

GO ON

Vocabulary-in-Context

Directions

When you read each of the sentences below, use the other words in the sentence to help you understand what the underlined word means. Then mark the correct space for the answer that you have picked.

Sample

Rather than quit, Jessica **persisted** and finally won the race. **Persisted** means —

Ⓐ stopped
● continued
Ⓒ pointed
Ⓓ stood

25 You will **neglect** your fish by not feeding it or not cleaning its tank. **Neglect** means —

Ⓐ train
Ⓑ spoil
Ⓒ ignore
Ⓓ protect

26 I was **concerned** about having to make a speech in front of a room of strangers. **Concerned** means —

Ⓕ smart
Ⓖ nervous
Ⓗ last
Ⓙ hurt

27 I set my alarm so I would not be **tardy** for school. **Tardy** means —

Ⓐ ready
Ⓑ surprised
Ⓒ late
Ⓓ absent

28 The **crucial** part of a movie is the scene that contains the key information. **Crucial** means —

Ⓕ most important
Ⓖ funniest
Ⓗ boring
Ⓙ last

29 I was **startled** by the late phone call last night. **Startled** means —

Ⓐ decided
Ⓑ passed
Ⓒ surprised
Ⓓ happy

30 The boy who was a **gifted** chess player won many contests. **Gifted** means —

Ⓕ shy
Ⓖ talented
Ⓗ small
Ⓙ beginner

STOP

Answer Sheet

1 (A) (B) (C) (D)
2 (F) (G) (H) (J)
3 (A) (B) (C) (D)
4 (F) (G) (H) (J)
5 (A) (B) (C) (D)
6 (F) (G) (H) (J)
7 (A) (B) (C) (D)
8 (F) (G) (H) (J)
9 (A) (B) (C) (D)
10 (F) (G) (H) (J)
11 (A) (B) (C) (D)
12 (F) (G) (H) (J)
13 (A) (B) (C) (D)
14 (F) (G) (H) (J)
15 (A) (B) (C) (D)

16 (F) (G) (H) (J)
17 (A) (B) (C) (D)
18 (F) (G) (H) (J)
19 (A) (B) (C) (D)
20 (F) (G) (H) (J)
21 (A) (B) (C) (D)
22 (F) (G) (H) (J)
23 (A) (B) (C) (D)
24 (F) (G) (H) (J)
25 (A) (B) (C) (D)
26 (F) (G) (H) (J)
27 (A) (B) (C) (D)
28 (F) (G) (H) (J)
29 (A) (B) (C) (D)
30 (F) (G) (H) (J)

Section 2: Reading Comprehension

50 Minutes

54 Questions

Directions: *Make sure you have a watch to time yourself and a No. 2 pencil. When you are ready, start timing yourself, and spend 50 minutes answering the questions in this section. Mark your answers on the Answer Sheet at the end of this section. If you are finished before the time is up, check over your work.*

Reading Comprehension

Directions

In this section, read the passages. Then pick the best answer for the questions that follow.

Sample

When Margarita heard the weather report predict a severe thunderstorm within the half hour, she began to worry how her younger brother would get home from his friend's house. Certainly he couldn't walk all those blocks in the rain.

Margarita's brother was —

Ⓐ doing his homework in his room
● at a friend's house
Ⓒ playing in the backyard
Ⓓ still at school

Carlos Sleeps Late

Carlos could never understand why his older brother Steve liked to sleep so much. He and Steve shared a bedroom, and every morning Carlos watched Steve do the same thing. Steve's alarm would go off, and his hand would shoot out to shut the alarm off. Then Steve would put his pillow over his head to drown out the noise of Carlos getting ready for school.

One Saturday morning, Carlos decided to stay in bed as long as Steve did. Carlos said, "I want to see what's so great about sleeping late everyday."

Steve laughed and said, "Sounds good to me!"

Carlos and Steve stayed in their beds. They listened to the rest of the family starting the day. Carlos heard his mother's voice. He strained to hear what

GO ON

she was saying. He smelled the good food cooking for breakfast. Carlos missed the busy life of the apartment in the morning. Steve was still sleeping in bed.

Carlos quietly said, "Can we get up yet? It sounds like there is fun stuff going on out there." Carlos waited a moment for Steve to respond, but Steve was silent. Carlos shouted, "Steve, my favorite cartoon is on in five minutes!"

Steve said, "Do what you want, Carlos. I'm staying in bed no matter how much I like cartoons." Carlos gave up. He went to the kitchen to eat breakfast and watch cartoons. Five minutes later, Steve joined Carlos in front of the television—with his pillow.

1 **Carlos wanted to —**

   Ⓐ get his brother's pillow

   Ⓑ stay in bed as long as his brother

   Ⓒ make breakfast for his family

   Ⓓ see what the plans were for the day

2 **What did Steve do when the alarm went off?**

   Ⓕ He got ready for school.

   Ⓖ He ate breakfast.

   Ⓗ He watched cartoons.

   Ⓙ He went back to sleep.

3 **The noise Carlos heard while in bed was —**

   Ⓐ the doorbell ringing

   Ⓑ traffic from outside

   Ⓒ his mother's voice

   Ⓓ the television

4 **Carlos got out of bed to —**

   Ⓕ go to school

   Ⓖ watch cartoons

   Ⓗ make sure he didn't miss the bus

   Ⓙ get away from his brother

5 **What will probably happen next?**

   Ⓐ The brothers will watch cartoons together.

   Ⓑ Carlos will go back to sleep.

   Ⓒ Steve won't want to sleep late anymore.

   Ⓓ Carlos will decide he doesn't like cartoons anymore.

GO ON

Park Rangers

A fun job for someone who likes to be outdoors is to be a park ranger. Park rangers enjoy nature, but they also have to work very hard. Their job is to protect the plants and animals that live in the park. Park rangers also make sure that the people who visit the park are safe. As you can see, it is a big job!

The first thing that a park ranger does in the morning is walk the paths of the park. The ranger keeps his or her eyes out for fallen trees or injured animals. Even in the rain, park rangers must do this. If the ranger finds an injured animal, the park might have to call a veterinarian, or animal doctor. This is the best way to bring an <u>ailing</u> animal back to health.

Caring for plants is another important part of a park ranger's job. Many park rangers will put labels next to interesting plants. The labels let people know what kinds of plants are in the park. Some plants are poisonous. The park ranger must make sure that visitors do not touch these plants. How will the park ranger do this? Well, park rangers often lead tours around the park to tell people about it. This is another part of the job that makes a park ranger an important person to nature and people alike.

GO ON

6 Another good title for this story is —

    Ⓕ "Helping the Plants"
    Ⓖ "The Animal Doctor"
    Ⓗ "Caring for the Park"
    Ⓙ "Labels for Plants"

7 This story was written in order to —

    Ⓐ tell about a job
    Ⓑ teach about animals
    Ⓒ give instructions
    Ⓓ list directions

8 Why does the writer tell about poisonous plants?

    Ⓕ To show how dangerous being a park ranger is
    Ⓖ To tell the different kinds of plants in a park
    Ⓗ To show that park rangers should wear gloves
    Ⓙ To show how park rangers must protect the visitors

9 You can tell that <u>ailing</u> means —

    Ⓐ friendly
    Ⓑ sick
    Ⓒ dangerous
    Ⓓ fun

10 The writer thinks that park rangers are —

    Ⓕ hard-working
    Ⓖ happy
    Ⓗ calm
    Ⓙ strong

GO ON

Jennifer and the Cats

Ever since Jennifer could remember, she wanted a cat as a pet. She had asked her mother many times, but her mother sneezed every time she was around animals. Because of her mother's sneezes, Jennifer thought she would never have a cat.

One night Jennifer thought she heard a "meow" outside her bedroom window. She listened very carefully for the sound again. All she could hear were cars and voices from the street below. "It must have been a dream," Jennifer said to herself. "I only heard the meow because I want a cat so badly." Jennifer sadly rolled over and went to sleep.

Jennifer found herself thinking about cats all the next day. She thought about big ones, little ones, striped ones, and spotted ones. She thought about whiskers and tails. With every cat, however, Jennifer remembered her mother's sneezes. Then Jennifer became sad again.

"Jennifer! Jennifer!" Her mother shook her awake the next night. "Listen!" Jennifer rubbed the sleep out of her eyes and listened to the noises outside. Suddenly, she heard the reason her mother had woken her up. There were meows coming from the stairs below the house. It sounded to Jennifer as though one hundred cats were crying.

Jennifer and her mother ran downstairs. They both stood in shocked silence at what they saw outside. Under the staircase was a mother cat and her seven new babies. The mother and baby cats all looked comfortable in the home they had made under the house. Jennifer had never seen anything so wonderful in her life.

"Can we keep them, mom? Please, can we?" Jennifer's mother thought for a second. Then she said, "Well, if they're outside, I guess I won't sneeze. Sure, we can keep them." Jennifer jumped around in joy. Her dreams to own a cat became true—eight times at once!

11 When Jennifer heard the meow at night, she was sad because —

    Ⓐ she thought it was a lost cat

    Ⓑ she thought the sound was a dream

    Ⓒ she knew the cat would not come inside

    Ⓓ she thought the cat was sick

12 What is another good name for this story?

    Ⓕ "A Sad Day at School"

    Ⓖ "Mother's Sneezes"

    Ⓗ "The Cat Surprise"

    Ⓙ "Noises from the Street"

13 Why did Jennifer's mother let her keep the cats?

    Ⓐ She no longer sneezed around animals.

    Ⓑ Jennifer asked her over and over again.

    Ⓒ The cats will live outside.

    Ⓓ She thought the cats would move away.

14 What will probably happen next?

    Ⓕ Jennifer will decide that she does not want the cats.

    Ⓖ Jennifer's mother will make the cats go away.

    Ⓗ The cats will move away because of the street noise.

    Ⓙ Jennifer will take care of the mother cat and her babies.

15 There is enough information in the story to show that —

    Ⓐ the baby cats were sick

    Ⓑ Jennifer also liked dogs

    Ⓒ Jennifer's mother hated animals

    Ⓓ the meow was not a dream

GO ON

Paper Snowflakes

Here's a fun and easy way to make snowflakes out of paper.

You will need:

White paper

Colored paper

A pair of scissors

Some string

Some glue

A garbage can

Instructions:

Fold the white paper in half. Then fold it in half again. Now fold it in half one more time. Next, take one corner of the paper and fold it to the opposite corner to form a triangle.

With your scissors, cut shapes from the sides of your folded paper. Make the shapes any size that you want. Make sure you put the pieces that you cut into the garbage can so you don't make a mess. When you are finished cutting, unfold the paper and look at your snowflake! Repeat these steps with the colored paper.

Line up your snowflakes and glue them to the string. Tie the string to the wall, and enjoy your paper snowflakes.

GO ON

16 The last step is to —

    (F) cut shapes from the paper

    (G) tie the string to the wall

    (H) fold the paper into a triangle

    (J) line up the snowflakes

17 The garbage can is used to —

    (A) carry the glue and string

    (B) help fold the paper

    (C) hold the pieces that you cut

    (D) separate the kinds of paper

18 Another good name for this project is —

    (F) "Snowflakes from Paper"

    (G) "Making Snowmen"

    (H) "Fun with Icicles"

    (J) "Christmas Trees"

19 How big should the shapes that you cut be?

    (A) One inch

    (B) Any size you want

    (C) Very small

    (D) Half an inch

20 If you wanted to find more ideas like this, you should —

    (F) look in a science book

    (G) visit a snowy mountain

    (H) look in an arts and crafts book

    (J) ask a weather expert

GO ON

The Violin

The violin is a very old instrument. A long time ago, kings and queens asked people to play the violin at parties. Then the guests would dance to the music. People also played the violin at concerts. Everyone in the town or village came to hear the concerts. The violin quickly became a favorite instrument of all the people. They liked the violin for its beautiful sound.

Today the violin is the same as it was two hundred years ago. It is made of wood and has four strings. Sometimes the wood is very special. Violins that are made out of special wood can be very expensive. Violin makers look for the *rare* wood, but it is very hard to find. Where do you think the wood comes from? It comes from trees, of course!

Violin players use something called a bow to make music. The bow is separate from the violin. A musician holds the violin in the left hand and the bow in the right hand. The bow goes across the violin strings to make sound. This takes a lot of practice. A good violin player must work very hard to make the music sound good.

Countries all over the world use the violin. Music in Mexico sounds very different from music in France. But both Mexico and France use the violin. The violin is also popular in the United States. Look for the violin the next time you go to a concert. You just might find it.

GO ON

21 Another good name for this story is —

Ⓐ "A Musical Instrument"
Ⓑ "Kings and Queens"
Ⓒ "Music in Mexico"
Ⓓ "Practice Makes Perfect"

22 This story was written in order to —

Ⓕ list directions
Ⓖ give instructions
Ⓗ teach about an instrument
Ⓙ tell about music around the world

23 Why does the writer tell about the bow?

Ⓐ To show that wood is expensive
Ⓑ To tell how people danced long ago
Ⓒ To show how the violin has changed
Ⓓ To show how the violin makes sound

24 You can tell that <u>rare</u> means —

Ⓕ made of wood
Ⓖ from another country
Ⓗ hard to find
Ⓙ sounding beautiful

GO ON

Clay Dough

Here's a fun and easy way to make your own clay dough.

Ingredients:

    1 cup flour

    $\frac{1}{2}$ cup salt

    1 tablespoon oil

    1 tablespoon alum (found in the spice section)

    1 cup boiling water (ask for help with this)

    food coloring

Instructions:

1. Combine flour, salt, oil, and alum in a large bowl.
2. Add the boiling water to the mixture and stir until a ball forms.
3. Add the food coloring.
4. Stir dough until it gets very sticky.
5. Store the dough in plastic bags in the refrigerator.

Yield:

Makes a 1-cup ball.

Recipe can be doubled.

GO ON

25 The last step is to —

    Ⓐ measure the salt
    Ⓑ store the dough in the refrigerator
    Ⓒ add the boiling water
    Ⓓ stir in the food coloring

26 The plastic bag is for —

    Ⓕ refrigerating the dough
    Ⓖ mixing the ingredients
    Ⓗ holding the food coloring
    Ⓙ storing the alum

27 The recipe tells you to ask for help with —

    Ⓐ picking the color you want
    Ⓑ stirring the mixture
    Ⓒ getting a bowl
    Ⓓ boiling the water

28 When will a ball form?

    Ⓕ When you double the recipe
    Ⓖ When you add the oil
    Ⓗ When you stir in the boiling water
    Ⓙ When you add the food coloring

29 Another good name for this activity is —

    Ⓐ "Make Your Own Clay Dough"
    Ⓑ "Food Coloring and Flour"
    Ⓒ "Colored Dough"
    Ⓓ "Food Art"

GO ON

SPORTING EVENTS

High School Football Game

Westbrook Field

Thursday, November 13

Gates open at 7:00 P.M.

Free for all students.

Adults $2.00

Sponsored by the Parents' Association

Town Track and Field Day

Memorial Field

Saturday, October 3

Arrive at 9:00 A.M. to participate.

Arrive at 11:00 A.M. to watch the events.

Call Debby Maloy for more information. 555-9271

Little League Championship

Come see the Ravens play the Junior Yanks!

Thursday, September 20 at 7:45 P.M.

Westbrook Field

Root for your favorite baseball team or just come for some fun and excitement.

A free barbecue will take place after the game. Everyone is invited.

Sponsored by Frank's Pizza

Soccer Tryouts

Westbrook High School Gym

Tuesday, September 18

Middle school at 3:00 P.M.

High school at 4:00 P.M.

Bring your cleats and shin guards.

Talk to Mr. Randall for more information. 555-9274

GO ON

30 Who should you call if you want to attend Town Track and Field Day?

- F Mr. Randall
- G Frank's Pizza
- H Debby Maloy
- J The Parents' Association

31 Which event will happen first?

- A Soccer Tryouts
- B High School Football Game
- C Little League Championship
- D Town Track and Field Day

32 These notices are most likely meant to be read by —

- F parents
- G students
- H teachers
- J coaches

33 Where did these notices probably appear?

- A A community newspaper
- B A baseball magazine
- C A telephone book
- D An encyclopedia

34 Where will the football game be held?

- F Memorial Field
- G Westbrook High School Gym
- H Westbrook Field
- J The notice does not say.

35 What event is having a barbecue afterwards?

- A Little League Championship
- B High School Football Game
- C Soccer Tryouts
- D Town Track and Field Day

36 At what time should a middle school student come to the soccer team tryouts?

- F 3:00 P.M.
- G 7:45 P.M.
- H 4:00 P.M.
- J 11:00 A.M.

37 Which of the following activities are students not encouraged to do?

- A Participate in sports
- B Join professional sports teams
- C Watch a sporting event
- D Support a favorite team

GO ON

The Largest Animal on Earth

You can't find the world's largest animal walking around on land. You have to look in the ocean because the largest animal on Earth is the blue whale.

A blue whale is usually between 75 and 80 feet long. The longest blue whale that we know about was 95 feet long. Blue whales usually weigh between 100 and 120 tons. Female whales are usually a little longer and heavier than males.

Blue whales can reach such enormous size because they live in the water. The water supports their great weight. The water also provides food for the whales. Blue whales eat tiny sea animals called "krill." A single whale can eat four tons of krill in a day.

Most blue whales travel to find their food. In the summer, they stay in the cold water of the Arctic or Antarctic Oceans. In the winter, they travel to warmer water. Baby blue whales, called "calves," are born while the whales are in the warmer water.

Blue whales make deep, rumbling noises that sound like moans. These sounds travel long distances. Blue whales can communicate with each other over hundreds of miles in the ocean.

In the past, blue whales were often hunted. There was so much hunting that the number of whales fell dramatically. Blue whales became an endangered species. Now people have agreed to stop hunting blue whales and to protect these giants of the ocean.

GO ON

38 This story was written mainly in order to —

    Ⓕ get you to protect blue whales

    Ⓖ tell you about blue whales

    Ⓗ describe how blue whales travel

    Ⓙ show that blue whales are dangerous

39 Why do blue whales make deep, rumbling noises?

    Ⓐ To find krill with echoes

    Ⓑ To scare away other animals

    Ⓒ To find their path in the ocean

    Ⓓ To communicate with other whales

40 Why do blue whales travel long distances?

    Ⓕ To see new places

    Ⓖ To find other whales

    Ⓗ To hear whale moans

    Ⓙ To get food

41 You would probably find this passage in a book called —

    Ⓐ "Animal Record Holders"

    Ⓑ "Visiting the Aquarium"

    Ⓒ "The Oceans of the World"

    Ⓓ "How Animals Travel"

42 If you wanted to know more about this animal, you should —

    Ⓕ get a whale as a pet

    Ⓖ visit a zoo

    Ⓗ look in an encyclopedia

    Ⓙ look up the word "whale" in a dictionary

43 The writer thinks that whales are —

    Ⓐ mean

    Ⓑ interesting

    Ⓒ funny

    Ⓓ shy

GO ON

Josh and the New Neighbors

Josh was looking out the window at his best friend Amir's old house. Amir didn't live there anymore. Josh missed Amir. Josh was feeling sad and lonely.

Suddenly he saw a small moving van come down the street. Maybe some new people were going to live in Amir's old house.

Josh rushed outside to see what would happen next. He saw the van stop in front of Amir's old house. Two men got out of the van and opened up the back doors. They set up a ramp and started moving some boxes and furniture into the house.

Josh looked carefully at the furniture for clues about who might be coming to live in the house. He saw a crib and guessed that the family must have a baby. But he didn't care much for babies.

"Too bad," Josh thought.

Then he saw one of the men lift up a bike. Josh was excited for a minute until he saw that the bike was small and pink. It looked just like his little sister's bike.

"Well, at least there will be somebody for Lisa to play with," he thought sadly.

Then Josh heard the sound of a car pulling up behind the moving van. He could see a family inside the car, but he couldn't tell exactly how many people were inside.

The back door of the car opened and a boy got out. He was just a little taller than Josh. The boy said, "Hi, I'm Eduardo. I guess you and I are going to be neighbors."

GO ON

KAPLAN

44 What problem does Josh have at the beginning of the story?

- Ⓕ He has to babysit for his little sister.
- Ⓖ His best friend has moved away.
- Ⓗ He had a fight with his friend Amir.
- Ⓙ His parents have told him to stay in his room.

45 Who does Josh first think is moving into Amir's house?

- Ⓐ A little girl
- Ⓑ A baby
- Ⓒ A boy his age
- Ⓓ Two men

46 Why did Josh think his sister would have someone to play with?

- Ⓕ He saw a car with the family.
- Ⓖ He saw a pink bicycle.
- Ⓗ He saw a crib.
- Ⓙ He saw a moving van.

47 Why does Josh look carefully at the furniture coming out of the truck?

- Ⓐ He hopes that his neighbors have a baby.
- Ⓑ His family collects furniture.
- Ⓒ He is hoping that a boy his age will move in.
- Ⓓ He thinks his friend Amir might return.

48 Another good title for this story would be —

- Ⓕ "The Pink Bicycle"
- Ⓖ "Josh's Friend Amir"
- Ⓗ "Furniture, Furniture, Furniture!"
- Ⓙ "Someone Is Moving In!"

49 Who were the two men who got out of the van?

- Ⓐ Amir's family
- Ⓑ Eduardo's brothers
- Ⓒ Movers for Eduardo's family
- Ⓓ Friends of Josh

50 What will probably happen next in the story?

- Ⓕ Josh will introduce himself.
- Ⓖ Josh and Eduardo will be best friends.
- Ⓗ Lisa will come to meet the new neighbors.
- Ⓙ Eduardo's family will tell him not to talk to Josh.

GO ON

How Rosie Found Her Dinner

Rosie the Raccoon woke up from her afternoon nap. She stretched her long back and shook her ringed tail. Then she said to herself, "I'm hungry. Where can I get something to eat?"

Rosie remembered that the bees had lots of delicious honey. She ran over to the beehive. When she asked the bees for some honey, they angrily buzzed, "We need our honey for ourselves." The bees wouldn't share any of their honey with Rosie.

"Maybe Sammy the Skunk has some nice old apples," thought Rosie. "I'm sure he would give me some." So Rosie headed over to Sammy's house. But as she got closer to the house, she noticed a smell that got worse and worse. It was almost enough to make her lose her appetite. Rosie decided to ask her friends at the ranger station for something to eat.

When Rosie got to the ranger station, she knocked politely on the front door. Nobody answered. "What a shame!" thought Rosie. "I'm sure the rangers would be happy to give me something. Maybe I'll check out back by the garbage pails."

Rosie scooted out back and lifted the lid off the garbage pail. Sure enough, the rangers had left her a very tasty snack.

GO ON

51 At the beginning of the story, Rosie feels —

- Ⓐ angry
- Ⓑ sad
- Ⓒ hungry
- Ⓓ happy

52 Where did Rosie go first?

- Ⓕ To the skunk's house
- Ⓖ To the beehive
- Ⓗ To the ranger station
- Ⓙ To the garbage pail

53 Why did Rosie quickly leave Sammy's house?

- Ⓐ Sammy was angry.
- Ⓑ There was a bad smell.
- Ⓒ She had stolen some food.
- Ⓓ Sammy was not home.

54 What will probably happen next?

- Ⓕ Rosie will eat something from the garbage pail.
- Ⓖ The rangers will come home and give Rosie some food.
- Ⓗ Sammy will invite Rosie to visit him.
- Ⓙ The bees will sting Rosie because she took their honey.

STOP

Answer Sheet

1	Ⓐ	Ⓑ	Ⓒ	Ⓓ		28	Ⓕ	Ⓖ	Ⓗ	Ⓙ
2	Ⓕ	Ⓖ	Ⓗ	Ⓙ		29	Ⓐ	Ⓑ	Ⓒ	Ⓓ
3	Ⓐ	Ⓑ	Ⓒ	Ⓓ		30	Ⓕ	Ⓖ	Ⓗ	Ⓙ
4	Ⓕ	Ⓖ	Ⓗ	Ⓙ		31	Ⓐ	Ⓑ	Ⓒ	Ⓓ
5	Ⓐ	Ⓑ	Ⓒ	Ⓓ		32	Ⓕ	Ⓖ	Ⓗ	Ⓙ
6	Ⓕ	Ⓖ	Ⓗ	Ⓙ		33	Ⓐ	Ⓑ	Ⓒ	Ⓓ
7	Ⓐ	Ⓑ	Ⓒ	Ⓓ		34	Ⓕ	Ⓖ	Ⓗ	Ⓙ
8	Ⓕ	Ⓖ	Ⓗ	Ⓙ		35	Ⓐ	Ⓑ	Ⓒ	Ⓓ
9	Ⓐ	Ⓑ	Ⓒ	Ⓓ		36	Ⓕ	Ⓖ	Ⓗ	Ⓙ
10	Ⓕ	Ⓖ	Ⓗ	Ⓙ		37	Ⓐ	Ⓑ	Ⓒ	Ⓓ
11	Ⓐ	Ⓑ	Ⓒ	Ⓓ		38	Ⓕ	Ⓖ	Ⓗ	Ⓙ
12	Ⓕ	Ⓖ	Ⓗ	Ⓙ		39	Ⓐ	Ⓑ	Ⓒ	Ⓓ
13	Ⓐ	Ⓑ	Ⓒ	Ⓓ		40	Ⓕ	Ⓖ	Ⓗ	Ⓙ
14	Ⓕ	Ⓖ	Ⓗ	Ⓙ		41	Ⓐ	Ⓑ	Ⓒ	Ⓓ
15	Ⓐ	Ⓑ	Ⓒ	Ⓓ		42	Ⓕ	Ⓖ	Ⓗ	Ⓙ
16	Ⓕ	Ⓖ	Ⓗ	Ⓙ		43	Ⓐ	Ⓑ	Ⓒ	Ⓓ
17	Ⓐ	Ⓑ	Ⓒ	Ⓓ		44	Ⓕ	Ⓖ	Ⓗ	Ⓙ
18	Ⓕ	Ⓖ	Ⓗ	Ⓙ		45	Ⓐ	Ⓑ	Ⓒ	Ⓓ
19	Ⓐ	Ⓑ	Ⓒ	Ⓓ		46	Ⓕ	Ⓖ	Ⓗ	Ⓙ
20	Ⓕ	Ⓖ	Ⓗ	Ⓙ		47	Ⓐ	Ⓑ	Ⓒ	Ⓓ
21	Ⓐ	Ⓑ	Ⓒ	Ⓓ		48	Ⓕ	Ⓖ	Ⓗ	Ⓙ
22	Ⓕ	Ⓖ	Ⓗ	Ⓙ		49	Ⓐ	Ⓑ	Ⓒ	Ⓓ
23	Ⓐ	Ⓑ	Ⓒ	Ⓓ		50	Ⓕ	Ⓖ	Ⓗ	Ⓙ
24	Ⓕ	Ⓖ	Ⓗ	Ⓙ		51	Ⓐ	Ⓑ	Ⓒ	Ⓓ
25	Ⓐ	Ⓑ	Ⓒ	Ⓓ		52	Ⓕ	Ⓖ	Ⓗ	Ⓙ
26	Ⓕ	Ⓖ	Ⓗ	Ⓙ		53	Ⓐ	Ⓑ	Ⓒ	Ⓓ
27	Ⓐ	Ⓑ	Ⓒ	Ⓓ		54	Ⓕ	Ⓖ	Ⓗ	Ⓙ

Section 3: Mathematics— Problem Solving

50 Minutes

46 Questions

Directions: *Make sure you have a watch to time yourself, a No. 2 pencil, and a ruler that has both metric and standard units. When you are ready, start timing yourself, and spend 50 minutes answering the questions in this section. Mark your answers on the Answer Sheet at the end of this section. If you are finished before the time is up, check over your work.*

Mathematics— Problem Solving

Directions

Read each question. Choose the best answer and mark that space.

Sample

Maria developed 24 pictures of her birthday party and 36 pictures of her sister's wedding. How many pictures did she develop all together?

Ⓐ 50

Ⓑ 59

● 60

Ⓓ 100

Ⓔ None

1 Mr. Green grew two thousand four hundred seventy-one pumpkins on his farm last year. Which choice shows this number?

Ⓐ 247,001

Ⓑ 24,701

Ⓒ 2,471

Ⓓ 271

2 Which choice shows one thousand six hundred eighty?

Ⓕ 168,000

Ⓖ 16,800

Ⓗ 1,680

Ⓙ 168

3 Mr. Smith drove 1,036 miles on a trip. What is the value of the 3 in 1,036?

Ⓐ three

Ⓑ thirty

Ⓒ three hundred

Ⓓ three thousand

4

THIRD GRADE BOOKS	
Book	Number of Pages
Math	546
Reading	510
English	394
Science	438

Which lists the books from the one with the fewest pages to the one with the most pages?

Ⓕ Math, Reading, English, Science

Ⓖ English, Reading, Science, Math

Ⓗ English, Science, Reading, Math

Ⓙ Reading, English, Math, Science

5 What number means 6,000 + 50 + 2?

Ⓐ 652

Ⓑ 6,052

Ⓒ 60,052

Ⓓ 650,002

GO ON

KAPLAN

6

School Candy Sale	
Grade	**Candy Bars Sold**
Grade 2	752
Grade 3	820
Grade 4	678
Grade 5	811

Which grade sold the most candy bars?

(F) Grade 2

(G) Grade 3

(H) Grade 4

(J) Grade 5

7 Which is another way to write 2 + 2 + 2?

(A) 2 + 2

(B) 2 − 2

(C) 2 × 3

(D) 2 ÷ 2

8 Which of the following is another way to write 8 + 8 + 8?

(F) 8 + 3

(G) 8 × 3

(H) 8 × 8 × 8 × 8

(J) 8 + 24

9 What number goes in the box and makes this number sentence true?

$1 \times \boxed{} = 13$

(A) 1

(B) 3

(C) 12

(D) 13

10 What number goes in the box and makes this number sentence true?

$4 \times 3 = 3 \times \boxed{}$

(F) 2

(G) 3

(H) 4

(J) 7

GO ON

11 Danny made a poster with frogs on it. $\frac{2}{4}$ of the frogs are darker than the others. Which could be the poster that Danny made?

Ⓐ

Ⓑ

Ⓒ

Ⓓ

12 What fraction of the pizza has been eaten?

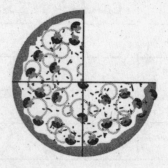

Ⓕ $\frac{1}{4}$

Ⓖ $\frac{1}{3}$

Ⓗ $\frac{1}{2}$

Ⓙ $\frac{3}{4}$

GO ON

KAPLAN

13 Barbara bought lime, orange, cherry, and apple jellybeans at the store. The table shows the fraction of each jellybean flavor eaten.

Jellybean Flavor	Amount Eaten
Lime	$\frac{1}{6}$
Orange	$\frac{1}{4}$
Cherry	$\frac{1}{2}$
Apple	$\frac{1}{8}$

Which jellybean flavor did she eat the most of?

Ⓐ Lime

Ⓑ Orange

Ⓒ Cherry

Ⓓ Apple

14 **Which fraction of the model is shaded?**

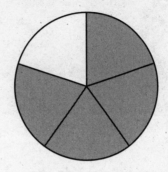

Ⓕ $\frac{1}{8}$

Ⓖ $\frac{4}{5}$

Ⓗ $\frac{4}{4}$

Ⓙ $\frac{2}{4}$

GO ON

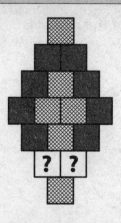

15 **Which squares below fit in the missing squares above?**

Ⓐ

Ⓑ

Ⓒ

Ⓓ

16 **A number machine produces numbers in a pattern. What will the next number be?**

 2, 5, 8, ___

Ⓕ 9

Ⓖ 11

Ⓗ 13

Ⓙ 14

17 **How many of these squares are necessary to make the figure below?**

Ⓐ 3

Ⓑ 4

Ⓒ 5

Ⓓ 8

GO ON

Lindsay made a tally chart showing the number of each type of coin in her bank. Use the tally chart to answer questions 18, 19, and 20.

LINDSAY'S COINS

Types of coins	Number of Coins
Pennies	☰☰☰ ☰☰☰ ☰☰☰ I
Nickels	☰☰☰ II
Dimes	☰☰☰ ☰☰☰
Quarters	☰☰☰ IIII
Half-Dollars	III

18 How many pennies does Lindsay have in her bank?

ⓕ 11

ⓖ 14

ⓗ 15

ⓙ 16

19 Lindsay has only 7 of which coins?

ⓐ Nickels

ⓑ Dimes

ⓒ Quarters

ⓓ Half-Dollars

20 Lindsay has three times as many of which coin as she does half-dollars?

ⓕ Pennies

ⓖ Nickels

ⓗ Dimes

ⓙ Quarters

GO ON

Claire, Monica, Quincy, Tom, Vikram, and Yuko compared the number of pets each one has. They recorded this information in a bar graph. Use the graph below to answer questions 21, 22, and 23.

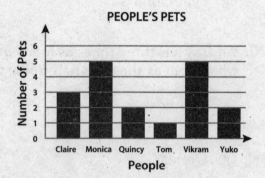

PEOPLE'S PETS

21 Which person has exactly 3 pets?

- Ⓐ Claire
- Ⓑ Monica
- Ⓒ Quincy
- Ⓓ Vikram

22 Which person has the fewest pets?

- Ⓕ Claire
- Ⓖ Quincy
- Ⓗ Tom
- Ⓙ Yuko

23 How many pets does Monica have?

- Ⓐ 3
- Ⓑ 4
- Ⓒ 5
- Ⓓ 6

24 Which has an end shaped like a square?

Ⓕ

Ⓖ

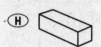
Ⓗ

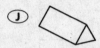
Ⓙ

25 Which is the location of the rabbit?

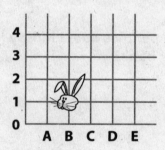

- Ⓐ B1
- Ⓑ B2
- Ⓒ C1
- Ⓓ C2

GO ON

26 You are looking for a number that is inside the circle. It is NOT inside the triangle. What is the number?

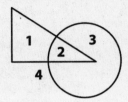

- Ⓕ 1
- Ⓖ 2
- Ⓗ 3
- Ⓙ 4

27 Which is the location of the dog?

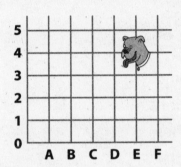

- Ⓐ E3
- Ⓑ E4
- Ⓒ F4
- Ⓓ F5

28 Which shape has three sides, all the same length?

Ⓕ

Ⓖ

Ⓗ

Ⓙ

29 You are looking for an odd number. It is inside the circle. It is NOT inside the triangle. It is inside the square. What is the number?

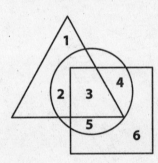

- Ⓐ 1
- Ⓑ 3
- Ⓒ 4
- Ⓓ 5

GO ON

30 Use your centimeter ruler for this question. How long is the pencil?

    Ⓕ 4 centimeters

    Ⓖ 5 centimeters

    Ⓗ 6 centimeters

    Ⓙ 7 centimeters

31 Use your inch ruler for this question.

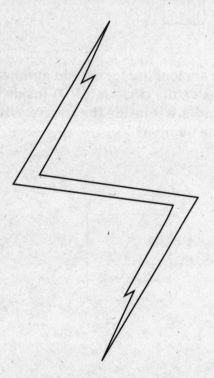

What is the total length of the lightning bolt in the picture?

    Ⓐ 4 inches

    Ⓑ 5 inches

    Ⓒ 6 inches

    Ⓓ 8 inches

32 On a hot summer day, Henry and Max got ice cream cones. Which was probably the temperature that day?

    Ⓕ 18° F

    Ⓖ 52° F

    Ⓗ 86° F

    Ⓙ 178° F

33 Chris weighed all the apples he picked in an orchard near his house. Which units can be used to measure weight?

    Ⓐ Pounds

    Ⓑ Gallons

    Ⓒ Inches

    Ⓓ Yards

34 Use your inch ruler for this question. How long is the key?

    Ⓕ 1 inch

    Ⓖ 2 inches

    Ⓗ 3 inches

    Ⓙ 4 inches

GO ON

35 After a big snowstorm, Sarah and her family built a snowman. Which was probably the temperature that day?

  (A) 24° F

  (B) 56° F

  (C) 71° F

  (D) 92° F

36 Use your centimeter ruler for this question. How tall is the cup?

  (F) 3 centimeters

  (G) 4 centimeters

  (H) 5 centimeters

  (J) 6 centimeters

37 Greg measured the height of a tomato plant in his backyard. Which units can be used to measure the plant's height?

  (A) Gallons

  (B) Pounds

  (C) Pints

  (D) Feet

38 Use your inch ruler for this question. How long is the button from one edge to the opposite edge?

  (F) 1 inch

  (G) 2 inches

  (H) 3 inches

  (J) 4 inches

39 Use your centimeter ruler for this question. How long is the sneaker?

  (A) 1 centimeter

  (B) 2 centimeters

  (C) 3 centimeters

  (D) 4 centimeters

GO ON

40 Georgeville is 327 miles from Franktown. What is that number rounded to the nearer hundred?

327 miles

Georgeville

Franktown

- (F) 300
- (G) 320
- (H) 330
- (J) 400

41 Ned bought these things at the toy store.

$1.10

$2.89

$4.03

About how much did he spend?

- (A) $6
- (B) $7
- (C) $8
- (D) $9

42 George sold these items at a garage sale.

$2.14

$0.85

$12.23

About how much did he make?

- (F) $10
- (G) $12
- (H) $15
- (J) $20

GO ON

43

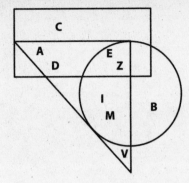

The secret letter is inside the rectangle. It is also inside the triangle. It is NOT inside the circle. The secret letter is a vowel. What is the secret letter?

Ⓐ A

Ⓑ Z

Ⓒ E

Ⓓ D

44 Ellen paid for a bag of chips with a one-dollar bill. To find out how much change she should receive, what else would you need to know?

Ⓕ How much the bag of chips cost

Ⓖ The name of the store

Ⓗ How long it took to eat the chips

Ⓙ The kind of chips she bought

45 Freddy decided to see if he could hop on one foot 450 times without stopping. He has hopped 220 times.

How many more times does he need to hop to reach his goal?

Ⓐ 190

Ⓑ 220

Ⓒ 230

Ⓓ 330

46 Alison bought 5 packs of her favorite gum. There are 8 pieces of gum in each pack.

How many pieces of gum did Alison buy in all?

Ⓕ 12

Ⓖ 20

Ⓗ 30

Ⓙ 40

STOP

Answer Sheet

1	(A)	(B)	(C)	(D)
2	(F)	(G)	(H)	(J)
3	(A)	(B)	(C)	(D)
4	(F)	(G)	(H)	(J)
5	(A)	(B)	(C)	(D)
6	(F)	(G)	(H)	(J)
7	(A)	(B)	(C)	(D)
8	(F)	(G)	(H)	(J)
9	(A)	(B)	(C)	(D)
10	(F)	(G)	(H)	(J)
11	(A)	(B)	(C)	(D)
12	(F)	(G)	(H)	(J)
13	(A)	(B)	(C)	(D)
14	(F)	(G)	(H)	(J)
15	(A)	(B)	(C)	(D)
16	(F)	(G)	(H)	(J)
17	(A)	(B)	(C)	(D)
18	(F)	(G)	(H)	(J)
19	(A)	(B)	(C)	(D)
20	(F)	(G)	(H)	(J)
21	(A)	(B)	(C)	(D)
22	(F)	(G)	(H)	(J)
23	(A)	(B)	(C)	(D)

24	(F)	(G)	(H)	(J)
25	(A)	(B)	(C)	(D)
26	(F)	(G)	(H)	(J)
27	(A)	(B)	(C)	(D)
28	(F)	(G)	(H)	(J)
29	(A)	(B)	(C)	(D)
30	(F)	(G)	(H)	(J)
31	(A)	(B)	(C)	(D)
32	(F)	(G)	(H)	(J)
33	(A)	(B)	(C)	(D)
34	(F)	(G)	(H)	(J)
35	(A)	(B)	(C)	(D)
36	(F)	(G)	(H)	(J)
37	(A)	(B)	(C)	(D)
38	(F)	(G)	(H)	(J)
39	(A)	(B)	(C)	(D)
40	(F)	(G)	(H)	(J)
41	(A)	(B)	(C)	(D)
42	(F)	(G)	(H)	(J)
43	(A)	(B)	(C)	(D)
44	(F)	(G)	(H)	(J)
45	(A)	(B)	(C)	(D)
46	(F)	(G)	(H)	(J)

Section 4: Mathematics— Procedures

30 Minutes

30 Questions

Directions: *Make sure you have a watch to time yourself, a No. 2 pencil, and a ruler that has both metric and standard units. When you are ready, start timing yourself, and spend 30 minutes answering the questions in this section. Mark your answers on the Answer Sheet that follows this section. If you are finished before the time is up, check over your work.*

Mathematics—Procedures

Directions

Read each question. Choose the best answer and mark that space. If you are certain that the answer is not here, mark NH.

Sample

$$151 + 120$$

- (A) 31
- (B) 251
- (C) 270
- ● 271
- (E) NH

1 $25 \div 5 =$

- (A) 4
- (B) 5
- (C) 6
- (D) 20
- (E) NH

2 46×10

- (F) 4610
- (G) 470
- (H) 461
- (J) 460
- (K) NH

3 $864 - 529$

- (A) 245
- (B) 334
- (C) 335
- (D) 345
- (E) NH

4 $89 + 47$

- (F) 136
- (G) 137
- (H) 1036
- (J) 1306
- (K) NH

5 Kathy had 145 stickers. If she bought 37 more, how many stickers would she have?

- (A) 37
- (B) 108
- (C) 172
- (D) 182
- (E) NH

GO ON

KAPLAN

6

$$933$$
$$-\,604$$

F 321
G 329
H 331
J 339
K NH

7 $7 \times 7 =$

A 49
B 42
C 35
D 14
E NH

8

$$56$$
$$239$$
$$+\,74$$

F 249
G 266
H 349
J 369
K NH

9 $2\overline{)16}$

A 9
B 8
C 7
D 6
E NH

10 Which will make this number sentence true if it is put in the box?

$$5 \times 2 = \boxed{} \times 5$$

F 2
G 5
H 10
J 12
K NH

11

$$139$$
$$+\,140$$

A 31
B 251
C 270
D 279
E NH

GO ON

12
$$\begin{array}{r} 66 \\ + 55 \\ \hline \end{array}$$

F 6655

G 1021

H 121

J 111

K NH

13
$$\begin{array}{r} 25 \\ 341 \\ + 63 \\ \hline \end{array}$$

A 429

B 448

C 654

D 976

E NH

14
$$\begin{array}{r} 62 \\ - 16 \\ \hline \end{array}$$

F 78

G 54

H 49

J 44

K NH

15
$$\begin{array}{r} 31 \\ \times 2 \\ \hline \end{array}$$

A 72

B 63

C 62

D 33

E NH

16
$$\begin{array}{r} 22 \\ \times 8 \\ \hline \end{array}$$

F 168

G 176

H 230

J 300

K NH

17
$$\begin{array}{r} 554 \\ \times 9 \\ \hline \end{array}$$

A 499

B 4536

C 4950

D 4986

E NH

18
$$\begin{array}{r} 57 \\ + 42 \\ \hline \end{array}$$

F 85

G 89

H 96

J 99

K NH

GO ON

19 Mr. Lidney's pool measures 128 feet in length. What is that number rounded to the nearer hundred?

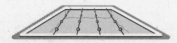

- Ⓐ 100
- Ⓑ 120
- Ⓒ 130
- Ⓓ 200
- Ⓔ NH

20 Harriet bought these items at the corner deli.

$5.89

$2.11 $3.06

<u>About</u> how much did she spend?

- Ⓕ $6
- Ⓖ $9
- Ⓗ $10
- Ⓙ $11
- Ⓚ NH

21 It's 347 miles between Southtown and Oceanville. What is that number rounded to the nearer ten?

347 miles

Southtown   Oceanville

- Ⓐ 300
- Ⓑ 340
- Ⓒ 350
- Ⓓ 400
- Ⓔ NH

22 Andy has three darts to throw at the dartboard below.

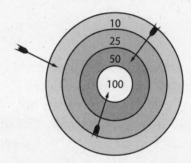

10
25
50
100

The first dart hits the 50-point ring, the second dart hits the 10-point ring and the last dart hits the 100-point ring. What is his total score?

- Ⓕ 70
- Ⓖ 150
- Ⓗ 160
- Ⓙ 250
- Ⓚ NH

GO ON

23 Francine made 70 cups of lemonade.

70

58

She sold 58 cups. How many cups did she have left?

Ⓐ 12

Ⓑ 18

Ⓒ 22

Ⓓ 52

Ⓔ NH

24 Nina practiced piano for 40 minutes on Monday, for 50 minutes on Tuesday, and for 60 minutes on Wednesday. How many minutes did she practice in all those three days?

Ⓕ 60 minutes

Ⓖ 120 minutes

Ⓗ 150 minutes

Ⓙ 180 minutes

Ⓚ NH

25 Sam's Stereo Store had a sale on CD players this week. The number of CD players sold each day is shown in the chart below.

Day of the Week	Number of CD Players Sold
Monday	11
Tuesday	45
Wednesday	53
Thursday	27
Friday	22
Saturday	57

On which day did the store sell twice as many CD players as they did on Monday?

Ⓐ Tuesday

Ⓑ Wednesday

Ⓒ Thursday

Ⓓ Friday

Ⓔ NH

GO ON

26 This tower has 246 stairs. I have already climbed 214 stairs.

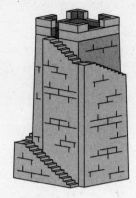

246

214

How many more stairs do I have left to climb?

- Ⓕ 32
- Ⓖ 42
- Ⓗ 122
- Ⓙ 232
- Ⓚ NH

27 Six children live on Queen Street. Each child has 3 pets. How many pets are there in all on Queen Street?

- Ⓐ 9
- Ⓑ 12
- Ⓒ 16
- Ⓓ 17
- Ⓔ NH

28 Stan has a lot of math homework to do. Each hour, Stan can do 13 math problems. If Stan does math problems for 3 hours, how many problems will he be able to do in all?

- Ⓕ 36
- Ⓖ 39
- Ⓗ 42
- Ⓙ 83
- Ⓚ NH

29 Walt has to write a story that is 120 words long. He has already written 65 words. How many more words does he have to write?

- Ⓐ 55
- Ⓑ 65
- Ⓒ 75
- Ⓓ 165
- Ⓔ NH

30 A librarian counted the number of people in a library one day. She counted 6 elementary school students, 14 middle school students and 8 adults. If no one else entered the library, how many people went to the library that day?

- Ⓕ 20
- Ⓖ 24
- Ⓗ 28
- Ⓙ 32
- Ⓚ NH

STOP

Answer Sheet

1	Ⓐ	Ⓑ	Ⓒ	Ⓓ	Ⓔ	16	Ⓕ	Ⓖ	Ⓗ	Ⓙ	Ⓚ
2	Ⓕ	Ⓖ	Ⓗ	Ⓙ	Ⓚ	17	Ⓐ	Ⓑ	Ⓒ	Ⓓ	Ⓔ
3	Ⓐ	Ⓑ	Ⓒ	Ⓓ	Ⓔ	18	Ⓕ	Ⓖ	Ⓗ	Ⓙ	Ⓚ
4	Ⓕ	Ⓖ	Ⓗ	Ⓙ	Ⓚ	19	Ⓐ	Ⓑ	Ⓒ	Ⓓ	Ⓔ
5	Ⓐ	Ⓑ	Ⓒ	Ⓓ	Ⓔ	20	Ⓕ	Ⓖ	Ⓗ	Ⓙ	Ⓚ
6	Ⓕ	Ⓖ	Ⓗ	Ⓙ	Ⓚ	21	Ⓐ	Ⓑ	Ⓒ	Ⓓ	Ⓔ
7	Ⓐ	Ⓑ	Ⓒ	Ⓓ	Ⓔ	22	Ⓕ	Ⓖ	Ⓗ	Ⓙ	Ⓚ
8	Ⓕ	Ⓖ	Ⓗ	Ⓙ	Ⓚ	23	Ⓐ	Ⓑ	Ⓒ	Ⓓ	Ⓔ
9	Ⓐ	Ⓑ	Ⓒ	Ⓓ	Ⓔ	24	Ⓕ	Ⓖ	Ⓗ	Ⓙ	Ⓚ
10	Ⓕ	Ⓖ	Ⓗ	Ⓙ	Ⓚ	25	Ⓐ	Ⓑ	Ⓒ	Ⓓ	Ⓔ
11	Ⓐ	Ⓑ	Ⓒ	Ⓓ	Ⓔ	26	Ⓕ	Ⓖ	Ⓗ	Ⓙ	Ⓚ
12	Ⓕ	Ⓖ	Ⓗ	Ⓙ	Ⓚ	27	Ⓐ	Ⓑ	Ⓒ	Ⓓ	Ⓔ
13	Ⓐ	Ⓑ	Ⓒ	Ⓓ	Ⓔ	28	Ⓕ	Ⓖ	Ⓗ	Ⓙ	Ⓚ
14	Ⓕ	Ⓖ	Ⓗ	Ⓙ	Ⓚ	29	Ⓐ	Ⓑ	Ⓒ	Ⓓ	Ⓔ
15	Ⓐ	Ⓑ	Ⓒ	Ⓓ	Ⓔ	30	Ⓕ	Ⓖ	Ⓗ	Ⓙ	Ⓚ

Section 5: Language

45 Minutes

48 Questions

Directions: Make sure you have a watch to time yourself and a No. 2 pencil. When you are ready, start timing yourself, and spend 45 minutes answering the questions in this section. Mark your answers on the Answer Sheet at the end of this section. If you are finished before the time is up, check over your work.

Language

Directions

Read each of the sentences below. Look at the underlined words in each sentence. There could be an error in punctuation, capitalization, or word usage. If you find an error in a sentence, pick the answer that is the best way to write the underlined words. If there is no error, pick "Correct as is."

Sample

He **must driven** to work every morning.

● must drive
Ⓑ must drove
Ⓒ must driving
Ⓓ Correct as is

1 Four boys from <u>dr. Greftor's</u> class will represent the school at the science fair.

Ⓐ Dr. Greftors
Ⓑ Dr. Greftor's
Ⓒ dr. Greftors
Ⓓ Correct as is

2 Paul <u>growed</u> more than three inches since last September.

Ⓕ grew
Ⓖ have grown
Ⓗ grows
Ⓙ Correct as is

3 The family went to <u>the Rocky mountains</u> on vacation.

Ⓐ the rocky mountains
Ⓑ The Rocky Mountains
Ⓒ the Rocky Mountains
Ⓓ Correct as is

4 I spoke to the teacher and <u>asked her about my grade?</u>

Ⓕ asking her about my grade?
Ⓖ asks her about my grade.
Ⓗ asked her about my grade.
Ⓙ Correct as is

5 Sometimes the man <u>coughed very loudly</u> when he takes his medicine.

Ⓐ coughing very loudly
Ⓑ coughs very loudly
Ⓒ cough very loudly
Ⓓ Correct as is

GO ON

6 <u>Amy and me wanted</u> to go to the movie last Wednesday.

    Ⓕ Amy and me wants

    Ⓖ Amy and I want

    Ⓗ Amy and I wanted

    Ⓙ Correct as is

7 The teacher <u>said, "You</u> may begin your homework if you are done with the assignment."

    Ⓐ said "You

    Ⓑ said, "you

    Ⓒ said "you

    Ⓓ Correct as is

9 Would you rather take <u>the train or the bus.</u>

    Ⓐ The Train or The Bus?

    Ⓑ the train or the bus?

    Ⓒ the Train or the Bus!

    Ⓓ Correct as is

8 When Carly <u>jump</u> into the pool, Branford will toss her the ball.

    Ⓕ jumps

    Ⓖ have jumped

    Ⓗ jumping

    Ⓙ Correct as is

10 We watched the <u>movie *Tarzan*</u> at the party.

    Ⓕ movie *tarzan*

    Ⓖ Movie *Tarzan*

    Ⓗ Movie *tarzan*

    Ⓙ Correct as is

GO ON

11 When the game was over, Ryan <u>said, "Let's</u> go home."

    Ⓐ said "Let's
    Ⓑ said, "lets
    Ⓒ said, Let's
    Ⓓ Correct as is

12 After the art class ended, the three brothers <u>draws</u> pictures.

    Ⓕ was drawing
    Ⓖ drew
    Ⓗ drawn
    Ⓙ Correct as is

13 The coach <u>said, We</u> have to practice harder."

    Ⓐ said, "we
    Ⓑ said We
    Ⓒ said, "We
    Ⓓ Correct as is

14 What is your favorite kind <u>of movie.</u>

    Ⓕ of movie?
    Ⓖ of Movie.
    Ⓗ of Movie!
    Ⓙ Correct as is

15 The fireman <u>said, "it</u> is safe to go inside."

    Ⓐ said, It
    Ⓑ said "it
    Ⓒ said, "It
    Ⓓ Correct as is

16 Ricky <u>and I were</u> on the same team.

    Ⓕ and me were
    Ⓖ and I was
    Ⓗ and me are
    Ⓙ Correct as is

17 Kristy <u>is the most best</u> athlete in the school.

    Ⓐ are the bestest
    Ⓑ is the best
    Ⓒ were the most best
    Ⓓ Correct as is

18 When Cindy <u>leave</u> the room, we will plan her party.

    Ⓕ leaves
    Ⓖ will leave
    Ⓗ left
    Ⓙ Correct as is

GO ON

Boxed Questions

Directions

Read the words in each of the boxes below. There could be an error in sentence structure. If you find an error in any group of words, pick the answer that is written most clearly and correctly. If there is no error, pick "Correct as is."

Sample

> My brother went to the store. To buy bread.

Ⓐ My brother went to the store buying bread.

⬤ My brother went to the store to buy bread.

Ⓒ To buy bread my brother went to the store.

Ⓓ Correct as is

19
> Felice handed me the book I took it from her.

Ⓐ Felice handed me the book, and I took it from her.

Ⓑ Felice handed me the book, I took it from her.

Ⓒ Felice handed me the book. I taking it from her.

Ⓓ Correct as is

20
> Two dogs in the car. They want to sit in the front seat.

Ⓕ There are two dogs in the car, they want to sit in the front seat.

Ⓖ Two dogs in the car want to sit in the front seat.

Ⓗ Two dogs in the car wanting to sit in the front seat.

Ⓙ Correct as is

21
> The dolphins jumped in the air after the trainer, she blew her whistle.

Ⓐ The dolphins jumped in the air after the trainer blew her whistle.

Ⓑ The dolphins jumped in the air after the trainer, and she blew her whistle.

Ⓒ After the trainer, she blew her whistle, the dolphins jumped in the air.

Ⓓ Correct as is

22
> Every morning, Sydelle tries to jog around the track.

Ⓕ She, Sydelle, tries to jog around the track every morning.

Ⓖ Sydelle, every morning, tries to jog around the track.

Ⓗ Around the track every morning Sydelle tries to jog.

Ⓙ Correct as is

 GO ON

23 | The bus traveled down the street. And turned left.

Ⓐ The bus traveling down the street and turning left.

Ⓑ The bus traveled down the street it turned left.

Ⓒ The bus traveled down the street and turned left.

Ⓓ Correct as is

24 | I asked for a piece of candy I got one.

Ⓕ I asked for a piece of candy, I got one.

Ⓖ I asked for a piece of candy. Me getting one.

Ⓗ I asked for a piece of candy, and I got one.

Ⓙ Correct as is

25 | The meal came with bread. And a salad.

Ⓐ The meal came with bread and a salad.

Ⓑ The meal came with bread, it came with a salad.

Ⓒ The meal coming with bread and a salad.

Ⓓ Correct as is

26 | The hockey player hit the puck into the goal.

Ⓕ The hockey player hit the puck. Into the goal.

Ⓖ The hockey player hitting the puck into the goal.

Ⓗ The hockey player hit the puck, and into the goal.

Ⓙ Correct as is

27 | My sister won an award, we celebrated with her.

Ⓐ My sister won an award. And celebrated with her.

Ⓑ My sister winning an award and celebrating with her.

Ⓒ My sister won an award, and we celebrated with her.

Ⓓ Correct as is

28 | Michael cut the bread. Into thin slices.

Ⓕ Michael cut the bread into thin slices.

Ⓖ Michael cut the bread he cut it into thin slices.

Ⓗ Michael cutting the bread into thin slices.

Ⓙ Correct as is

GO ON

KAPLAN

Directions

Read the paragraph, then answer the questions that follow.

Sample

Dear Aunt Elizabeth,

Thank you for the coins you sent me. How did you know that I needed a 1913 penny to complete my collection? I am so happy.

I hope you will come visit us soon.

Your niece,
Sarah

What is the best topic sentence for this paragraph?

Ⓐ When will you visit?

● Thank you for the coins.

Ⓒ Do you have any nickels?

Ⓓ Coin collecting is fun.

GO ON

Paragraph 1

Penguins are birds that do not fly. They have wings and feathers, but they never manage to get off the ground. Penguins live in cold areas like the North Pole. Penguins live in families just like humans. Adult penguins teach baby penguins how to swim and catch fish. You can watch this if you go to a zoo that has penguins.

29 Which of these would not belong in this paragraph?

Ⓐ Penguin feathers are black and white.

Ⓑ Penguin families are usually quite large.

Ⓒ The beak on a penguin is very small.

Ⓓ Another bird that does not fly is the ostrich.

30 Which of these would be the best topic sentence for this paragraph?

Ⓕ Penguins are interesting animals with many different features.

Ⓖ Many zoos have penguins that are nice to look at.

Ⓗ Even though penguins do not fly, their wings serve other purposes.

Ⓙ Penguins live in cold areas because their feathers protect them.

31 Which of these would go best after the last sentence?

Ⓐ Penguin feathers are slick with oil to help them swim.

Ⓑ Many zoos in the area have penguins for you to see.

Ⓒ Penguins eat small fish that they catch in the icy water.

Ⓓ Penguins must swim quickly because they do not fly.

32 For which group was this paragraph most likely written?

Ⓕ People who study penguins for a living

Ⓖ People who live at the North Pole

Ⓗ People who want to learn about penguins

Ⓙ Experts on birds that do not fly

GO ON

KAPLAN

Paragraph 2

Chantelle visited her grandmother in New Orleans. She had a great time on the trip. Chantelle and her grandmother heard a live jazz band. They ate spicy food. They also took a steamboat ride on the Mississippi River. Chantelle took pictures of her grandmother at all the places they visited. She wanted to remember her trip forever.

33 How could the first two sentences best be combined?

Ⓐ Chantelle visiting her grandmother in New Orleans and having a great time on the trip.

Ⓑ Chantelle visited her grandmother in New Orleans, and she had a great time on the trip.

Ⓒ Visiting her grandmother in New Orleans, and Chantelle had a great time on the trip.

Ⓓ In New Orleans Chantelle visited her grandmother, a great time on the trip.

34 Which of these would not belong in this paragraph?

Ⓕ Another fun place to visit is Seattle.

Ⓖ Chantelle also visited some art galleries.

Ⓗ It was the best vacation Chantelle ever had.

Ⓙ Chantelle's grandmother took her all over the city.

35 What is the main reason this paragraph was written?

Ⓐ To tell you to go somewhere
Ⓑ To make you laugh
Ⓒ To give a map of a city
Ⓓ To describe a girl's trip

GO ON

Paragraph 3

Dear Uncle Pete,

Thank you very much for the gift you sent me for my birthday. How did you know that I collect baseball cards? The baseball card that you sent me is very nice. I have been looking for it for a long time. I would like to show you my cards the next time you visit. Please let me know when that will be.

Sincerely,
Betsy

36 What is the main reason this letter was written?

- Ⓕ To tell about a baseball card
- Ⓖ To thank someone for a gift
- Ⓗ To ask a question
- Ⓙ To find out about a visit

37 Which of these would not belong in this paragraph?

- Ⓐ The baseball card is a perfect fit with my collection.
- Ⓑ I did not know that you are interested in baseball cards.
- Ⓒ The athlete on the card is one of my favorite players.
- Ⓓ I also collect model airplanes made out of wood.

38 Which of these would go best after the last sentence in this paragraph?

- Ⓕ Baseball cards are a great thing to collect.
- Ⓖ I tried to buy that card at a shop, but it cost too much.
- Ⓗ I hope you visit soon because I miss you.
- Ⓙ The card is rare because only a few were made.

GO ON

KAPLAN

Directions

Read each question below. Pick the best answer for each one. Then mark the correct space for the answer that you have picked.

Sample

Look at these guide words from a dictionary page.

> hero — house

Which word could be found on the page?

- Ⓐ heart
- Ⓑ humid
- ● high
- Ⓓ hurt

39 Look at these guide words from a dictionary page.

> crock — cycle

Which word could be found on the page?

- Ⓐ class
- Ⓑ cure
- Ⓒ court
- Ⓓ city

40 Look at these guide words from a dictionary page.

> fence — fly

Which word could be found on the page?

- Ⓕ farm
- Ⓖ fast
- Ⓗ fry
- Ⓙ fit

41 Look at these guide words from a dictionary page.

> park — pen

Which word could be found on the page?

- Ⓐ pin
- Ⓑ play
- Ⓒ pat
- Ⓓ pray

42 If you want to find out about the results of a town meeting yesterday, you should look in —

- Ⓕ a history book
- Ⓖ a local newspaper
- Ⓗ an atlas
- Ⓙ an encyclopedia

GO ON

43 If you want to know the meaning of a word, you should look in —

    Ⓐ an almanac

    Ⓑ a dictionary

    Ⓒ an encyclopedia

    Ⓓ an atlas

44 If you want to find information about the first president of the United States, you should look in —

    Ⓕ a dictionary

    Ⓖ a newspaper

    Ⓗ an encyclopedia

    Ⓙ an atlas

45 To find out the population of India, you should look in —

    Ⓐ a language arts book

    Ⓑ a dictionary

    Ⓒ a newspaper

    Ⓓ an almanac

46 Which of these is a main heading that includes the other three words?

    Ⓕ Painting

    Ⓖ Art

    Ⓗ Sculpture

    Ⓙ Drawing

47 Which of these is a main heading that includes the other three words?

    Ⓐ Pants

    Ⓑ Shirt

    Ⓒ Clothes

    Ⓓ Sock

48 Which of these is a main heading that includes the other three words?

    Ⓕ Pets

    Ⓖ Cat

    Ⓗ Fish

    Ⓙ Dog

STOP

Answer Sheet

1	A	B	C	D		25	A	B	C	D
2	F	G	H	J		26	F	G	H	J
3	A	B	C	D		27	A	B	C	D
4	F	G	H	J		28	F	G	H	J
5	A	B	C	D		29	A	B	C	D
6	F	G	H	J		30	F	G	H	J
7	A	B	C	D		31	A	B	C	D
8	F	G	H	J		32	F	G	H	J
9	A	B	C	D		33	A	B	C	D
10	F	G	H	J		34	F	G	H	J
11	A	B	C	D		35	A	B	C	D
12	F	G	H	J		36	F	G	H	J
13	A	B	C	D		37	A	B	C	D
14	F	G	H	J		38	F	G	H	J
15	A	B	C	D		39	A	B	C	D
16	F	G	H	J		40	F	G	H	J
17	A	B	C	D		41	A	B	C	D
18	F	G	H	J		42	F	G	H	J
19	A	B	C	D		43	A	B	C	D
20	F	G	H	J		44	F	G	H	J
21	A	B	C	D		45	A	B	C	D
22	F	G	H	J		46	F	G	H	J
23	A	B	C	D		47	A	B	C	D
24	F	G	H	J		48	F	G	H	J

Section 6: Spelling

25 Minutes

30 Questions

Directions: *Make sure you have a watch to time yourself and a No. 2 pencil. When you are ready, start timing yourself, and spend 25 minutes answering the questions in this section. Mark your answers on the Answer Sheet at the end of this section. If you are finished before the time is up, check over your work. This is the last section of the test.*

Spelling

Directions

Read each set of sentences below. Determine whether one of the underlined words in the set is spelled incorrectly or whether there is "No mistake." Then mark the correct space for the answer that you have picked.

Sample

● John is <u>finnishing</u> his homework.
Ⓑ Sarah has <u>gone</u> to the soccer game.
Ⓒ Jim worked on his <u>computer</u> for several hours.
Ⓓ No mistake

1 Ⓐ My dog did a <u>trick</u>.
Ⓑ The book was <u>eazy</u> to read.
Ⓒ Diane is a good <u>swimmer</u>.
Ⓓ No mistake

2 Ⓕ The <u>window</u> is open.
Ⓖ I was <u>afraid</u> of the lion.
Ⓗ Ari is <u>eigt</u> years old.
Ⓙ No mistake

3 Ⓐ We crossed the <u>brige</u>.
Ⓑ Doug spilled some <u>glue</u>.
Ⓒ Amy was <u>proud</u> of her work.
Ⓓ No mistake

4 Ⓕ Rick <u>wore</u> a new cap.
Ⓖ Do you want anything <u>elese</u>?
Ⓗ Where did you go in <u>town</u>?
Ⓙ No mistake

5 Ⓐ Gail <u>said</u> she was sorry.
Ⓑ David read the <u>whole</u> book.
Ⓒ Alyssa <u>would</u> like to go with us.
Ⓓ No mistake

6 Ⓕ The belt is too <u>loose</u>.
Ⓖ There are sixty seconds in one <u>minute</u>.
Ⓗ We <u>allways</u> eat a good breakfast.
Ⓙ No mistake

GO ON

KAPLAN

7
  Ⓐ Corn is my favorite <u>vegtable</u>.
  Ⓑ The team plays <u>once</u> a week.
  Ⓒ The teacher told us to be <u>quiet</u>.
  Ⓓ No mistake

8
  Ⓕ Did the storm <u>destroy</u> the house?
  Ⓖ She lives <u>across</u> the street from me.
  Ⓗ Come tomorrow <u>instead</u> of Friday.
  Ⓙ No mistake

9
  Ⓐ He went to see the <u>docter</u>.
  Ⓑ What <u>caused</u> the fire?
  Ⓒ She runs a small <u>business</u>.
  Ⓓ No mistake

10
  Ⓕ Henry has a bad <u>cough</u>.
  Ⓖ We <u>know</u> how to skate.
  Ⓗ The car <u>stoped</u> at the light.
  Ⓙ No mistake

11
  Ⓐ I need glasses to see <u>beter</u>.
  Ⓑ Buy a <u>thick</u> coat to wear in winter.
  Ⓒ He was in a <u>hurry</u> to get there.
  Ⓓ No mistake

12
  Ⓕ I need a babysitter this <u>Saturday</u> night.
  Ⓖ I can't wait until summer <u>vacasion</u>.
  Ⓗ Nick <u>promised</u> he'd be good.
  Ⓙ No mistake

13
  Ⓐ The shirt had too many <u>buttons</u>.
  Ⓑ I was careful when I <u>poured</u> the juice.
  Ⓒ The city is very <u>bright</u> at night.
  Ⓓ No mistake

GO ON

14 Ⓕ She <u>seemed</u> to think it was funny.
Ⓖ She used a <u>nife</u> to cut the meat.
Ⓗ My uncle lives in the <u>country</u>.
Ⓙ No mistake

15 Ⓐ I hope I can get a <u>bicycle</u>.
Ⓑ There was <u>nothing</u> else to do.
Ⓒ The bag had strong <u>handels</u>.
Ⓓ No mistake

16 Ⓕ I like to play right <u>field</u> in baseball.
Ⓖ I've never been horseback <u>rideing</u>.
Ⓗ <u>Cereal</u> is my favorite breakfast food.
Ⓙ No mistake

17 Ⓐ I <u>slippt</u> in the mud.
Ⓑ It was a <u>heavy</u> rain.
Ⓒ <u>Boil</u> water to make tea.
Ⓓ No mistake

18 Ⓕ The rain <u>cauzed</u> a mudslide.
Ⓖ Shiqua will <u>hurry</u> back to class.
Ⓗ The grass on the <u>field</u> is green.
Ⓙ No mistake

19 Ⓐ Spencer is my <u>neighber</u>.
Ⓑ Did she <u>understand</u> the problem?
Ⓒ My favorite <u>flavor</u> is vanilla.
Ⓓ No mistake

20 Ⓕ We are <u>ready</u>.
Ⓖ He wrote his <u>adress</u>.
Ⓗ She put the <u>money</u> away.
Ⓙ No mistake

21 Ⓐ Hang your <u>scarf</u> in the closet.
Ⓑ All the <u>buses</u> leave here at eight o'clock.
Ⓒ I cannot <u>remember</u> her name.
Ⓓ No mistake

GO ON

22
  Ⓕ She was <u>happy</u>.
  Ⓖ The house is <u>very</u> old.
  Ⓗ The moon was <u>brigt</u>.
  Ⓙ No mistake

23
  Ⓐ He felt <u>tired</u>.
  Ⓑ <u>Shugar</u> tastes sweet.
  Ⓒ The club meets on <u>Wednesday</u>.
  Ⓓ No mistake

24
  Ⓕ <u>Tell</u> me the story.
  Ⓖ Jorge is a good <u>friend</u>.
  Ⓗ The dog has soft <u>fur</u>.
  Ⓙ No mistake

25
  Ⓐ We had a <u>buzy</u> day.
  Ⓑ I will see him <u>tonight</u>.
  Ⓒ She has <u>something</u> to say.
  Ⓓ No mistake

26
  Ⓕ <u>Which</u> jacket is yours?
  Ⓖ How <u>meny</u> players are on the team?
  Ⓗ Does anybody know the <u>answer</u>?
  Ⓙ No mistake

27
  Ⓐ Jody tried to do it <u>again</u>.
  Ⓑ Kevin <u>wrote</u> a letter to his cousin.
  Ⓒ Fran said she was <u>truely</u> sorry.
  Ⓓ No mistake

28
  Ⓕ Christmas is my <u>favorite</u> day.
  Ⓖ David <u>blushs</u> when nervous.
  Ⓗ <u>Traffic</u> is bad today.
  Ⓙ No mistake

29
  Ⓐ The supplies were <u>plentifull</u>.
  Ⓑ He <u>shied</u> away from us.
  Ⓒ The puzzle was <u>simple</u>.
  Ⓓ No mistake

30
  Ⓕ The teacher <u>repeats</u> herself.
  Ⓖ Do not go <u>below</u> deck.
  Ⓗ Monday is a <u>holliday</u>.
  Ⓙ No mistake

STOP

Answer Sheet

1 (A) (B) (C) (D)
2 (F) (G) (H) (J)
3 (A) (B) (C) (D)
4 (F) (G) (H) (J)
5 (A) (B) (C) (D)
6 (F) (G) (H) (J)
7 (A) (B) (C) (D)
8 (F) (G) (H) (J)
9 (A) (B) (C) (D)
10 (F) (G) (H) (J)
11 (A) (B) (C) (D)
12 (F) (G) (H) (J)
13 (A) (B) (C) (D)
14 (F) (G) (H) (J)
15 (A) (B) (C) (D)

16 (F) (G) (H) (J)
17 (A) (B) (C) (D)
18 (F) (G) (H) (J)
19 (A) (B) (C) (D)
20 (F) (G) (H) (J)
21 (A) (B) (C) (D)
22 (F) (G) (H) (J)
23 (A) (B) (C) (D)
24 (F) (G) (H) (J)
25 (A) (B) (C) (D)
26 (F) (G) (H) (J)
27 (A) (B) (C) (D)
28 (F) (G) (H) (J)
29 (A) (B) (C) (D)
30 (F) (G) (H) (J)

PRACTICE TEST **A**

Answer Key

Reading Vocabulary

1	B
2	F
3	D
4	F
5	B
6	G
7	A
8	H
9	A
10	G
11	A
12	H
13	C
14	J
15	B
16	H
17	B
18	G
19	C
20	J
21	A
22	J
23	B
24	H
25	C
26	G
27	C
28	F
29	C
30	G

Reading Comprehension

1	B	28	H
2	J	29	A
3	C	30	H
4	G	31	D
5	A	32	G
6	H	33	A
7	A	34	H
8	J	35	A
9	B	36	F
10	F	37	B
11	B	38	G
12	H	39	D
13	C	40	J
14	J	41	A
15	D	42	H
16	G	43	B
17	C	44	G
18	F	45	B
19	B	46	G
20	H	47	C
21	A	48	J
22	H	49	C
23	D	50	F
24	H	51	C
25	B	52	G
26	F	53	B
27	D	54	F

Mathematics—Problem Solving

1	C	24	H
2	H	25	A
3	B	26	H
4	H	27	B
5	B	28	G
6	G	29	D
7	C	30	F
8	G	31	C
9	D	32	H
10	H	33	A
11	B	34	G
12	F	35	A
13	C	36	F
14	G	37	D
15	D	38	F
16	G	39	C
17	B	40	F
18	J	41	C
19	A	42	H
20	J	43	A
21	A	44	F
22	H	45	C
23	C	46	J

Mathematics—Procedures

1	B
2	J
3	C
4	F
5	D
6	G
7	A
8	J
9	B
10	F
11	D
12	H
13	A
14	K
15	C
16	G
17	D
18	J
19	A
20	J
21	C
22	H
23	A
24	H
25	D
26	F
27	E
28	G
29	A
30	H

Language

1	B	25	A
2	F	26	J
3	C	27	C
4	H	28	F
5	B	29	D
6	H	30	F
7	D	31	C
8	F	32	H
9	B	33	B
10	J	34	F
11	D	35	D
12	G	36	G
13	C	37	D
14	F	38	H
15	C	39	B
16	J	40	J
17	B	41	C
18	F	42	G
19	A	43	B
20	G	44	H
21	A	45	D
22	J	46	G
23	C	47	C
24	H	48	F

Spelling

1	B
2	H
3	A
4	G
5	D
6	H
7	A
8	J
9	A
10	H
11	A
12	G
13	D
14	G
15	C
16	G
17	A
18	F
19	A
20	G
21	D
22	H
23	B
24	J
25	A
26	G
27	C
28	G
29	A
30	H

Answers and Explanations for Practice Test A

Answers and Explanations for Practice Test A

 **Reading Vocabulary**

Questions 1–18: Synonyms

Synonym questions make up most of the Reading Vocabulary section. Here, you have to pick the word or phrase that means the same thing as the underlined word. While it would be good to know each of the words, you should not worry if you don't. When you see a word you don't know, remember this fact:

> You do not need to know the exact dictionary definition of a word. If you have a general idea of its definition, that should be enough to help you cross out some answer choices and guess.

Try thinking about words in terms of *positive/negative (good/bad)*. For example, say you don't exactly know what the word *acclaim* means. However, you do know that it means something positive. You can now go to the answer choices and eliminate any negative answer choices. There's no way a positive word will have a negative synonym.

Question 1   *Elect* is a positive word, so choice **C** can be crossed out, since *catch* is not really positive. The answer is **B**.

Question 2   If you are *certain* of a fact, then you know that it is true. The answer is **F**.

Question 3   Again, *applaud* is positive—think of an audience that *applauds* a show—so **B** could be crossed out. If you think of an audience *applauding*, this should lead you to **D**, *clap*.

Question 4   *Giggle* is positive, and this makes **G**, *book*, not a good choice, since *book* doesn't really have either a positive or negative meaning. The answer is **F**.

Question 5   A good way to work on this question is to think of a way the word *private* is often used, such as *private property*. Since *private property* usually means "owned by one person or family," the answer is **B**.

Question 6   Although the question asks for the meaning of the word *invent*, the words *inventor* and *invention* could help you figure out the answer to this question. An inventor *creates* something new, so **G** is correct.

Question 7   **A** is correct.

Question 8   An adjective, *narrow* means something *slender*, *slim*, or *thin*, choice **H**. Since there are people who are thin and also tall—think of models, for instance—choice **G** has been placed to catch people who think narrow means *tall*.

Question 9   Thinking of the word *confess* and how it is often used will help on this problem. Criminals who are guilty sometimes *confess* their crimes, while priests of some religions listen to *confession*. Thinking about these two instances will lead you to **A**, *admit*.

Question 10   The answer is **G**.

Question 11   In school, if a student is *absent*, he or she is not at school. **A**, *not here*, is the correct choice.

Question 12   If you or your parents belong to any clubs or *organizations*, this should be simple. The answer is **H**. Well-known *organizations* include the U.N. (United Nations) and the P.T.A. (Parent—Teachers' Association).

Question 13   A common use of *sketch* is in the phrase *sketch artist*. A sketch artist is a person employed by police to *draw*—choice **C**—the face of a suspected criminal.

Question 14   **J** is correct. Think of trading, or *swapping*, baseball cards.

Question 15   **B** is correct.

Question 16 When the weather is *chilly*, it is cold outside, so this would mean the best answer for the problem is **H**.

Question 17 For those who think of the phrase "drifting with the tides," two choices look good. **A** and **B** are both good guesses, but **B** is the correct synonym for *drift*.

Question 18 This is a difficult word, since *summit* is used in more than one way often. A summit can be an important meeting, but it is also the highest part of a mountain, so in this case **G** is correct.

Questions 19–24: Multiple Meaning Questions

Here's a good way of working on these questions: Try to figure out the part of speech of the underlined word in the boxed sentence. For example, say you decide that the underlined word in the boxed sentence is a noun. You can now cross out any answer choices that do not use the underlined word as a noun. This should leave with 1–3 choices left to choose from.

Question 19 In the boxed-in sentence, *load* is used as a verb that means to *fill*. **A** and **D** both use *load* as a noun, so they can be crossed out. **C** is the correct answer.

Question 20 In this example, *by* means *next to* or *near*. In choice **J**, the house is *near* the school.

Question 21 In the boxed-in sentence, *honor* is used as a noun. **C** can be crossed out since it uses *honor* as a verb. In the boxed sentence and choice **A**, *honor* means an *award*.

Question 22 Since *ring* is used as a noun in the boxed sentence, **H** can be crossed out since it uses *ring* as a verb. **J** is the answer.

Question 23 **B** must be the answer, as it is the only choice that uses *watch* as a verb. **C** and **D** have *watch* as a noun, while **A** uses it as an adjective.

Question 24 **F** and **J** can be crossed out as they have *back* as a noun. **H** is correct.

Questions 25–30: Context

The best way to do these questions is a simple one: Read the sentence and use clues within the sentence to figure out what the underlined word means. Next, go to the answer choices and find the word that is closest to the definition you came up with.

Question 25 *Neglect* must be a negative word, as the sentence shows how someone who *neglects* their fish does not feed them or clean their tank. **C** is correct.

Question 26 Most people would be worried about making *a speech in front of strangers*, so *concerned* must be worried or *nervous*, choice **G**.

Question 27 You would *set an alarm* in order to get somewhere on time, so not *tardy* is closest to not *late*, **C**.

Question 28 The best clue in this sentence seems to be *key information*, and this means that *crucial* is closest to **F**, *most important*.

Question 29 Since late phone calls are not common, most people would not expect them. This would lead people to be *surprised* (**C**), or *startled*, when they receive such a call.

Question 30 Since the boy *won many contests*, he had to know what he was doing. The answer is **G**.

Reading Comprehension

The best approach to Reading Comprehension passages is to read the passage through once to understand the main point. Then, head for the questions but *constantly* go back to the passage in order to make sure you have the correct answer. Many students try to answer the questions from memory, since they feel this saves time. While it may save a few seconds, it also leads to wrong answers. Remember, the answers are in the passage. Since the passage is always there for you to use, it's very important to keep going back to it. That way, you will always be able to find the right answer choice.

Question 1 The answer to this question can be found in the second paragraph. It gives you the main idea of the entire story: Carlos is going to try to sleep as late as his brother. The answer is **B**.

Question 2 Although choice **H** eventually happens, in the first paragraph it states that Steve turns off the alarm clock when he hears it and then goes back to sleep (**J**).

Question 3 Choices **A** and **B** are not mentioned anywhere in the passage, which leaves **C** and **D**. While Carlos does at one point watch cartoons, he doesn't watch them in bed. The best answer in this problem is **C**, which is stated in the fourth paragraph.

Question 4 Choice **G** is correct, as the fifth paragraph states why Carlos finally left his bed.

Question 5 The last few sentences of the passage will give you a good idea of the correct answer. There is no reason to choose **C** or **D**. **B** is true—Carlos will have to sleep again sometime!—but it is not the answer. The best response is **A**, since Steve has joined his brother in front of the TV.

Question 6 Understanding the main idea of a passage will lead you to the correct answer here. While **J** is mentioned in the third paragraph, it is not the main idea of the passage. It is merely one thing that a park ranger does while taking care of the park, choice **H**.

Question 7 This is another question for which knowing the main idea is important. Since all three paragraphs talk about what a park ranger does, the answer is **A**.

Question 8 Right after the sentence "Some plants are poisonous," it states that the park ranger needs to "make sure that visitors do not touch these plants." **J** is correct.

Question 9 This question is like the Context questions in Reading Vocabulary, so you can see that the test-taking strategies you learned for one part of the test can be used in the other parts. In the sentence before *ailing animal*, the same animal is described as *injured*. This means that *ailing* is a negative word, which crosses out **A** and **D**. Choice **B**, *sick*, is closer to *injured* than *dangerous*.

Question 10 Only choice **F** can be found in the passage (look at the second sentence).

Question 11 The information needed to answer this question correctly can be found in the second paragraph. After hearing the "meow" Jennifer states, "It must have been a dream." Choice **B** is correct.

Question 12   G is talked about, but the story is not about Jennifer's mother's sneezing. Choice **H** is the only answer that has the word *cat* in it. Since this is a story about cats, that should be a good clue that this is the correct response.

Question 13   While choice **B** is stated in the first paragraph, the correct response comes from the mother's statement in the final paragraph. Since the cats will live outside, Jennifer's mother lets them stay. Choice **C**.

Question 14   Jennifer's desire to have a cat is stated several times during the passage. The best response is **J**.

Question 15   **D** is the best response.

Question 16   To look for a correct answer to a question that asks about "the last step," you should look at the end of the passage. While the passage ends with *enjoy your paper snowflakes*, this is not given as a choice. If it were, it would be the correct response. However, the statement right before it, *tie the string to the wall*, is choice **G**, and it's the correct response.

Question 17   The answer here is choice **C**, and it can be found in the second paragraph of the instructions.

Question 18   This is a main idea question, but clues can be found from the very beginning, as the passage is titled "Paper Snowflakes." Choice **F** is correct.

Question 19   Going back to the passage, you can find this answer in the second sentence of the second paragraph. Choice **B** is correct.

Question 20   This problem asks you to think about the passage as a whole, and what this activity really is. They aren't real snowflakes, so **G** and **J** are not correct. Instead, making paper snowflakes is more of an art project (choice **H**), which is why the passage tells you to hang them on the wall when you are finished.

Question 21   The main idea of this passage is a discussion of the violin. Since the violin is a musical instrument, **A** is the correct response. **B** and **C** are phrases mentioned in the passage, but they do not state the main idea.

Question 22   If you answered question 21 correctly, you should get **H** on this problem as well, since it is also asking about the main idea.

Question 23   Going back to the passage, the third paragraph talks about how the *bow goes across the violin to make sound*. **D** is the answer.

Question 24   Reading after the phrase *rare wood*, the passage noted that this wood is *hard to find*, choice **H**.

Question 25   Looking at Instruction 5 in the middle of the page, the fifth step is to *store the dough*, choice **B**.

Question 26   Reading the fifth instruction again, you can see that the refrigerated dough is kept in plastic bags, so **F** is the answer.

Question 27   Choice **B** is the fourth step of the instructions, but it doesn't say anything about asking for help. However, in the *Ingredients* portion of the passage, it says that you should ask for help boiling the water, **D**.

Question 28   Answer **H** can be found as the second step of the Instructions.

Question 29   While both **A** and **C** contain the key word *dough*, **A** is the better answer since making the dough is a better description (coloring the dough is only one part of the project).

Question 30   There's no main idea on this functional passage, but there are clues to help you find the correct answer quickly. Since this question mentions *Town Track and Field Day*, you should immediately head to that paragraph to start searching for the answer. **H** is correct.

Question 31   You will have to look at each of the four events to find the answer. However, you need to find only the starting times. Then, all you have to do is compare the times to find **D** is the correct answer. Choice **B** looks good until you realize that it is in the P.M., while the track and field competition takes place in the A.M.

Question 32   This is a tougher question, but the best clue can be found in the *Soccer Tryouts* section. Since it says *bring your cleats and shin guards*, the notice is probably meant for the students, **G**. Also, under *High School Football Game*, it says *free for all students*.

Question 33   While the Little League Championship could appear in a baseball magazine (**B**), the other notices would not. The correct answer is choice **A**.

Question 34   Heading to the correct section, *High School Football Game*, will lead you to choice **H**.

Question 35   Answer **A** is correct.

Question 36   The phrase *soccer team tryouts* would lead you to the proper box. **F** and **H** are both choices, but since the question refers to *middle school* only, **F** is correct.

Question 37   Process of elimination works well here. Cross out every answer choice that is mentioned somewhere in the notice. This leaves you with **B**.

Question 38   Every answer choice contains the key phrase *blue whales*. However, the passage is about many different things about the blue whale (size, eating habits, etcetera). **G** is correct.

Question 39   In the fifth paragraph, the passage describes how these sounds are used to communicate with other whales, choice **D**.

Question 40   The first sentence of the fourth paragraph states the blue whales travel to find food, **J**.

Question 41   The key here is the title of the passage, *The Largest Animal on Earth*. This points to **A**, the correct answer.

Question 42   **F** and **G** are not correct because of the large size of blue whales. **H** is the answer, since **J** would only give the definition and spelling of "whale."

Question 43   Questions that ask what the writer thinks usually have positive answers. This is because the reading passages are usually educational and interesting. This eliminates **A**, and of the three choices left, **B** is the best answer.

Question 44 From the first two sentences of the first paragraph, you can see that Josh is sad because his best friend Amir has moved away. The answer is **G**.

Question 45 Although the *two men* are mentioned before anyone else (they appear in the third paragraph), the fact that the family arrives in a car in the eighth paragraph means that these two men are only movers. The first person Josh thinks is moving in is a baby, choice **B**, since the two men move a crib into the house in paragraph four.

Question 46 The pink bicycle in the sixth paragraph looks like his sister's bike, so Josh guesses that his sister might have a playmate. **G** is the answer.

Question 47 Since you know from question 44 that Josh misses his best friend, a good response on this question is **C**, since Josh is hoping someone his age will move in.

Question 48 The answer to this main idea question is **J**.

Question 49 Since question 45 made you realize that the two men were movers, this problem should be fairly simple. **C** is correct.

Question 50 The best response is **F**. Eduardo introduces himself, so it would be logical for Josh to do the same.

Question 51 The first paragraph states how Rosie is hungry after her nap, **C**. Also, since the main idea of this passage is something like "Rosie searches for food," this should have lead you to **C** as well.

Question 52 Looking at the passage, the second paragraph shows Rosie first visited the bees, **G**.

Question 53 From the third paragraph, the answer is **B**.

Question 54 Since the last sentence has Rosie discovering a tasty snack in the garbage pail, you can make a good guess that she will now eat the food, choice **F**.

Mathematics—Problem Solving

This is the first of two Math sections, Math—Procedures being the other one. In Problem Solving, almost all of the questions ask you to do some reading, so be ready to answer some problems with more than one step. Some of the problems may take 2–3 minutes to work on.

Questions 1–6: Number Sense and Numeration

These questions test how well you understand numbers.

Question 1   **C** is the correct answer. Sometimes, using only part of the number can help you use process of elimination (POE for short). For example, in this question the last two digits are seventy-one. Looking at the answer choices, only **C** and **D** have the correct last two digits. This would allow you to cross out **A** and **B** and take a guess.

Question 2   **H**.

Question 3   **B** is the correct answer.

Question 4   POE can be used here. Once you see that English has the fewest pages at 394, you can go to the answer choices and cross out any choice that doesn't start with English. This leaves only **G** and **H**. Since Science has the next fewest pages, **H** is correct.

Question 5   **B** is correct. Students in a hurry might choose **A**, missing the three zeroes on *6,000*.

Question 6   **G**.

Questions 7–10: Whole Number Computation

These questions test how well you understand basic facts about addition, subtraction, multiplication, and division.

Question 7   Multiplication can be used to shorten this addition problem. The answer is **C**, as both equations equal 6.

Question 8   **G** is correct.

Question 9   Since any number multiplied by 1 remains the same number, the missing number in the box must be 13, **D**.

Question 10   There are two ways to solve this. In the first, you just do the math: 4 x 3 on the left side equals 12, so now you know that 3 x (missing number) must equal 12 as well. The other is knowing that 4 x 3 = 3 x 4, no matter what order they are in. The answer is 4, **H.**

Questions 11–14: Fractions and Decimal Concepts

These questions test how well you understand fractions and decimals.

Question 11   2/4 is the important fraction. You want to look for a group of four frogs which has two dark frogs. This group would represent the fraction 2/4. The answer is **B.**

Question 12   The pizza has been cut into four sections, but one section has been eaten, so the answer is **F.**

Question 13   Since the top numbers in the chart are all equal (1), the choice with the smallest bottom number will be the largest fraction. The answer is **C.**

Question 14   Similar to the pizza question, there are five sections (the whole of the group), and four of the sections are shaded (the part of the group), so the answer is **G.**

Questions 15–17: Patterns and Relationships

These questions test how well you understand patterns, including pictures and numbers. For math patterns, you can often use addition or subtraction to find the answer.

Question 15   The figure is symmetrical. This means that if you fold the figure in half, the top and bottom would look the same. Since the two cubes on the top half of the figure are both dark, the bottom two cubes would be dark as well. **D.**

Question 16   Adding 3 to the last number is how this pattern works. This means the number after 8 will be 8 + 3 = 11, choice **G.**

Question 17   **B** is correct.

Questions 18–23: Statistics and Probability

These questions often use a chart or graph of some form. Knowing about the different kind of charts and graphs is the best way to do well on these questions.

Question 18   Reading across the top of the chart where the word *Pennies* is, you should count 16 scratch marks, choice **J**.

Question 19   **A** is the answer.

Question 20   This is a two-step problem. First, find the number of half–dollars Lindsay has. She has 3 half-dollars. Now look for the coin that has 3 times this number; you are looking for 9 coins. Lindsey has 9 quarters, so **J** is the answer.

Question 21   **A** is correct.

Question 22   Look for the smallest bar, which must be the person who has the fewest pets. The answer is Tom, **H**.

Question 23   Monica has 5 pets, so **C** is the answer.

Questions 24–29: Geometry and Spatial Sense

These questions cover problems with basic shapes like squares, triangles, and circles. There are also questions that ask you to find the coordinates of an object on a graph.

Question 24   Although **G** has a four-sided end, it is in the shape of a rectangle. In order to be a square, all four sides must be of equal length, so the answer is **H**.

Question 25   Reading horizontally, the rabbit is directly above letter B. Therefore, choices **C** and **D** can be eliminated because they do not start with B. The rabbit is directly across from the number 1, so the answer is choice **A**.

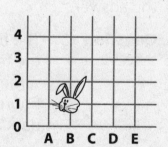

Question 26   **H** is the answer.

Question 27   Similar to the rabbit question, the dog is directly above the letter E and directly across from the number 4, so E4, choice **B**, is the answer.

Question 28   Only **F** and **G** have three sides, but **F** has sides of different length, so the correct choice is **G**.

Question 29   POE can be very helpful here. The first part of the question says you are looking for an odd number. This gets rids of **C**, 4. The next clue states it is inside the circle: 1 is not inside the circle, so **A** can be crossed out. The next clue says it is NOT inside the triangle, and since 3 is inside the triangle, choice **B** can be crossed off. This leaves only **D**, so it must be the correct answer. By using POE, you did not even have to look at the last clue.

Questions 30–39: Measurement

The largest group of questions in this section is Measurement. Many of these questions just ask you to use your ruler and measure a drawing or shape. Other Measurement questions include counting change, comparing lengths, and using the right units (feet instead of gallons, for example).

Question 30   The pencil is 4 cm, choice **F**. If you got the wrong answer on this question, make sure you look at where the 0 is on your ruler. Some people start measuring from the end of the ruler, but this is not always where the zero is. You need to begin measuring from where the zero is.

Question 31   Switching to inches, each section of the bolt is two inches, and since there are three sections, 2+ 2 + 2 = 6 inches, **C**.

Question 32   Although **F** might be a good answer choice in Celsius units, choice **H**—86 degrees Fahrenheit—describes a hot summer day.

Question 33   The only unit present that measures weight is *pounds*, **A**.

Question 34   The answer is **G**.

Question 35   Since snow usually melts at temperatures above 32 degrees Fahrenheit, the best answer for this question is **A**.

Question 36   **F** is correct.

Question 37   The only unit present that could measure *height* is feet, **D**.

Question 38   Since the question asks for the length in inches, the answer is **F**. If you mistakenly used centimeters when measuring, you could end up with either **G** or **H**.

Question 39   Since length would be measured from the heel of the shoe to the tip, the answer is **C**.

Question 40–42: Estimation

These questions test how well you can round off numbers to estimate the answers.

Question 40 327 rounded to the nearest *hundred* is 300, since 327 is closer to 300 than 400. **F** is correct.

Question 41 First, you should round $1.10 to $1, $2.89 to $3, and $4.03 to $4 Then, $1 + $3 + $4 = $8, choice **C**.

Question 42 Using the same steps as you did on question 41, you should get $15, **H**.

Questions 43–46: Problem Solving Strategies

There are many different question types in this group. Some use the same skills you've already learned taking the other parts of the test.

Question 43 POE is effective on this problem. The first two clues, that the secret letter is inside the rectangle and triangle, do not eliminate any choices. However, the third clue, that the letter is NOT inside the circle, gets rids of choices **B** and **C**. Since the secret letter is a vowel, the answer is **A**.

Question 44 **F** is the key missing factor.

Question 45 Since Freddie has hopped 220 times, if you subtract this number from 450, you will find out how many hops he has left to do. The answer is **C**, 230.

Question 46 Multiplying 5 packs x 8 pieces (the number of pieces in each pack) yields 40, choice **J**, which is the total number of bubble gum pieces.

Mathematics—Procedures

Over half of the questions in this section are just math problems. A key to answering these questions correctly is to write down all your work. Trying to answer these questions in your head often leads to careless errors, and you lose points on questions that you really do know how to do. So write down your work!

There are five possible answer choices on this section, not four as in the other parts of the test. The fifth choice is always NH, which stands for Not Here. If you work a problem and then do not find the answer in the first four choices, work the problem again. If you get the same answer the second time, pick NH and move on to the next question.

Question 1   B.

Question 2   J.

Question 3   C.

Question 4   F.

Question 5   If Kathy bought 37 more stickers, you need to add that number to the amount of stickers she already has, 145. 145 + 37 = 182, choice **D**.

Question 6   G.

Question 7   A.

Question 8   J.

Question 9   B.

Question 10   F.

Question 11   D.

Question 12   H.

Question 13   A.

Question 14   K. Here's an example of an answer that is *Not Here*, NH.

Question 15   C.

Question 16   G.

Question 17   D.

Question 18   J.

Questions 19–21: Rounding

These questions are like the Estimation questions in the Math—Problem Solving section.

Question 19 Since the number must be rounded to the nearest hundred, the answer is **A**, since 128 is closer to 100 than 200.

Question 20 First, you need to round $2.11 to $2, $5.89 to $6, and $3.06 to $3. Adding $2 + $6 + $3 = $11, choice **J**.

Question 21 Rounded to the nearer *ten*, the answer is **C**.

Questions 22–30: Computation in Context

These questions are mainly word problems. The key is to read the question carefully, and then decide what math operation—addition, subtraction, multiplication, or division—you need to do to get the correct answer.

Question 22 To find Andy's total score, the three dart scores must be added up, so 50 + 10 + 100 = 160, choice **H**.

Question 23 After selling 58 cups, Francine would have 70 – 58 = 12 cups left, **A**.

70

Question 24 To find her total number of practice minutes, the numbers need to be added, so 40 + 50 + 60 = 150 minutes, choice **H**.

58

Question 25 First, you need to read the chart correctly to find the number of CDs sold on Monday. That number, 11 must then be multiplied by 2 since you are looking for the day that had twice Monday's sales. You then look for 22 on the chart, and find it next to Friday. **D** is correct.

Question 26 Usually when the question uses the phrase *have left*, subtraction is needed. 246 – 214 = 32 steps left, choice **F**.

Question 27 If six kids have three pets each, then 6 x 3 = 18 pets total. Since the number 18 does not appear in the first four choices, the answer must be **E**, Not Here.

Question 28   You could use either addition or multiplication to get at the right answer. Realizing he does 13 questions per hour for 3 hours, 13 x 3 = 39. You could also think 13 + 13 + 13 = 39. The answer is **G**.

Question 29   Having already written 65 words, he has 120 – 65 = 55 words remaining, **A**.

Question 30   To find the total number of people, add 6 + 14 + 8 = 28 people in all, **H**.

Language

This section tests your knowledge of grammar. Most of the questions test how well you understand punctuation, capitalization, and how to form sentences. Common errors include uncapitalized proper nouns, misplaced or missing commas, and improper subject-verb agreement.

Many students don't like grammar tests much. Still, remember this is a multiple-choice test. You don't necessarily have to be perfect at grammar—you just need to be able to spot incorrect grammar when you see it.

Each question in this section has four choices, and the fourth answer on the first 28 questions is always "Correct as is." If you look at a question and can find no error, reread the question carefully. If you still don't find an error, simply pick *Correct as is* and move on.

Questions 1–18: Capitalization, Punctuation, and Usage

These questions have underlined phrases that may or may not have errors in punctuation, capitalization, and word usage. The goal is to find the error, and then choose the answer choice that corrects the mistake.

Question 1   Since *dr. Greftor* refers to a specific person, the *Dr.* should be capitalized. The apostrophe is correctly used. **B**.

Question 2   This is the incorrect past tense of the verb *grow*: *grew* is correct. **F**.

Question 3   As the *Rocky Mountains* are a specific place, they need to be capitalized. However, "the" is just an article and not part of the name, so the correct answer is **C**.

Question 4   The person speaking is not asking a question, so the question mark is incorrect. A period is correct. **H**.

Question 5   *Coughed* is in the past tense, but the event is not in the past. The answer is *coughs*, present tense. **B**

Question 6   Since the pronoun *me* is part of the subject, it should be *Amy and I wanted*, choice **H**.

Question 7   Correct as is. **D**.

Question 8   The verb *jump* is missing an *-s*. **F**.

Question 9   Since the sentence is asking a question, there needs to be a question mark at the end. However, the train or bus are not proper nouns, so they are not capitalized. **B**.

Question 10   Correct as is. **J**.

Question 11   Correct as is. **D**.

Question 12   *Draws* is not in the past tense, and it does not agree with the subject *brothers*. The correct form is *drew*, **G**.

Question 13   Since the coach is speaking, there need to be quotation marks at both the beginning and the end of his statement. **C**.

Question 14   This sentence is a question, so **F** is correct.

Question 15   The first word within the quotation, it, needs to be capitalized. **C**.

Question 16   Correct as is. **J**.

Question 17   The word *best* is all that is needed to explain that someone is the top athlete, so adding *most* is wrong. **B**.

Question 18   This is a subject-verb agreement problem that can be fixed by adding an *-s* to the end of the verb. **F**.

Question 19–28: Sentence Structure

These questions include boxed–in sentences that sometimes contain errors. The goal is to find the error and then choose the answer choice that fixes the problem. If you find no error, pick *Correct as is*.

Question 19   Since this a compound sentence, it needs the conjunction *and* a comma to combine the two parts. **A.**

Question 20   The first part is a sentence fragment, but it can be combined with the second part to form choice **G.**

Question 21   The pronoun *she* and the comma are not needed. They can be eliminated. **A.**

Question 22   Correct as is. **J.**

Question 23   The phrase *And turned left* is fragment that needs to be combined with the rest of the sentence. **C.**

Question 24   This question has the same problem as question 19, and can be solved the same way. **H.**

Question 25   *And a salad* is a sentence fragment that must be combined with the first sentence. **A.**

Question 26   Correct as is. **J.**

Question 27   The two parts of this sentence are missing a conjunction such as *and*. **C** is correct.

Question 28   This question has the same problem as question 25 and can be solved the same way. **F.**

Question 29–38: Content and Organization

These questions are similar to Reading Comprehension questions. You read a minipassage and then answer questions about the text. Like the Reading Comprehension passages, read these passages once to get the main idea, then head for the questions. Go back to the passage constantly as you answer the questions. There is sometimes a grammar question in this section as well.

Question 29   **D** does not fit into the main idea of the passage, which is about penguins.

Question 30 The best expression of the main idea is **F**. Choice **H** is true, but it is not the main idea.

Question 31 Although **B** talks about zoos, which is a word in the last sentence, the end of the passage is talking about penguins swimming and catching fish. Because of this, **C** is the best answer.

Question 32 **H** is correct.

Question 33 This problem is like a Sentence Structure question. The best way to combine the sentences is to add the conjunction *and* along with a comma. **B**.

Question 34 Seattle has nothing to do with the passage, so **F** is the answer.

Question 35 The answer to this main idea–type question is **D**.

Question 36 The answer is **G**, which can be seen in the fact that the first part of the letter's body is *Thank you very much for the gift*.

Question 37 Model airplanes have nothing to do with athletes or baseball cards, so **D** is correct.

Question 38 Since the last part of the letter is talking about his uncle's next visit, the answer is **H**.

Questions 39–48: Study Skills

This category tests your knowledge of reference materials, such as dictionaries and encyclopedias. There are also several problems concerning proper alphabetizing.

Question 39 **B**.

Question 40 **J**.

Question 41 **C**.

Question 42 Since newspapers often have a section about local events, **G** is the best answer.

Question 43 Dictionaries provide spellings and explanations of unknown words. **B**.

Question 44 An encyclopedia—which would contain passages on historical events, places, and people (in addition to other facts)—is the best answer for this question. **H.**

Question 45 Almanacs contain information about world population, so **D** is correct.

Question 46 Painting, sculpture, and drawing are all different kinds of *art*. **G.**

Question 47 Pants, shirts, and socks are all parts of a person's *clothes*. **C.**

Question 48 Cats, dogs, and fish are all different kinds of *pets*. **F.**

Spelling

Each of the thirty spelling questions has four answer choices. In the first three answer choices, one of the words in each sentence will be underlined. If you believe that any of these words are incorrectly spelled, that choice is the answer for that question. If you look over the first three choices and believe all the words are spelled correctly, then you must pick the fourth choice, which is always No mistake.

Having a large vocabulary is the best way to do well on the Spelling section. However, knowing how to add suffixes (such as the *-es* at the end of suffixes) is also an important skill, as many spelling errors occur when suffixes are incorrectly added.

Question 1 *Eazy* is spelled *easy*. **B.**

Question 2 *Eigt* is spelled *eight*. **H.**

Question 3 *Brige* is spelled *bridge*. **A.**

Question 4 *Elese* is spelled *else*. **G.**

Question 5 No Mistake. **D.**

Question 6 *Allways* is spelled *always*. **H.**

Question 7 *Vegtable* is spelled *vegetable*. **A.**

Question 8 No Mistake. **J.**

Question 9 *Docter* is spelled *doctor*. **A.**

Question 10 *Stoped* is spelled *stopped*. **H.**

Question 11   *Beter* is spelled *better*. **A**.

Question 12   *Vacasion* is spelled *vacation*. **G**.

Question 13   No Mistake. **D**.

Question 14   *Nife* is spelled *knife*. **G**.

Question 15   *Handels* is spelled *handles*. **C**.

Question 16   *Rideing* is spelled *riding*. **G**.

Question 17   *Slippt* is spelled *slipped*. **A**.

Question 18   *Cauzed* is spelled *caused*. **F**.

Question 19   *Neighber* is spelled *neighbor*. **A**.

Question 20   *Adress* is spelled *address*. **G**.

Question 21   No Mistake. **D**.

Question 22   *Brigt* is spelled *bright*. **H**.

Question 23   *Shugar* is spelled *sugar*. **B**.

Question 24   No Mistake. **J**.

Question 25   *Buzy* is spelled *busy*. **A**.

Question 26   *Meny* is spelled *many*. **G**.

Question 27   *Truely* is spelled *truly*. **C**.

Question 28   *Blushs* is spelled *blushes*. **G**.

Question 29   *Plentifull* is spelled *plentiful*. **A**.

Question 30   *Holliday* is spelled *holiday*. **H**.

Test-Taking Strategies

Now you've taken the first test, and are getting ready to take the second. Before you do, take a look at this section. You will learn some special skills for answering each type of question. You will also find these strategies and tips in the **Answers and Explanations** section for Practice Test A. In this chapter, we've summarized them for you. Spend some time studying these skills before you start the second test.

Some general strategies you should keep in mind as you look at the different kinds of questions:

- Use *process of elimination*: Crossing out answers you know are wrong is called process of elimination. You eliminate, or get rid of, the incorrect answers to find the right one.

- Always answer every question, even if you have to guess. You don't get any points subtracted for guessing, but you do get a point if you are right!

- Don't get stuck on any one question. Do the questions you can first. You can always go back to the harder ones.

Let's take a look at each question type. Remember, you can use the above strategies throughout the test.

Reading Vocabulary

Synonyms

Synonyms, or words that mean the same thing, are a big part of the vocabulary section. The key here is not to get upset if you see a word you don't know. You don't always need to know the exact meaning of a word to get the question right. If you have some idea of what the word means (or doesn't mean), that can help you cross out some answer choices and guess.

Remember, you can make a good guess by asking if the word is *positive* (good) or *negative* (bad). For example, say you don't exactly know what the word *congratulate* means. However, you do know that *congratulate* means something good. You can then go to the answer choices and cross out any answer choices that seem to mean something bad. A positive word won't have a negative synonym. (The opposite is also true, of course.)

Multiple Meanings

The correct answer here has to be the same part of speech as the underlined word in the boxed sentence. For example, let's say you think that the underlined word in the boxed sentence is used as a noun. Then you can cross out any answer choices that use the underlined word as a verb or adjective. This should leave you with 1–3 choices left to choose from. Remember, the more choices you can cross out, the better your odds of answering the question correctly.

Vocabulary-in-Context

For these questions, just read the sentence, then use the other words in the sentence to understand the meaning of the underlined word. Next, go to the answer choices and find the word that is closest to the definition you came up with.

Reading Comprehension

The best way to do these questions is to read the passage to understand the main point. Next, head to the questions. However, you should *frequently go back* to the passage in order to make sure you have the correct answer. You may think it will waste time to keep looking at the passage, but it won't in the long run. The answers are in the passage, so why risk a wrong answer? Since you can always look at the passage, use it to find the best answer choice.

Mathematics—Problem Solving

Here, you will find some problems that may have two or more steps. They may take 2–3 minutes to work on. Others can be done faster. Remember that you don't get points subtracted for guessing on any part of the Stanford 9 tests. Therefore, you should always answer every question, even if you are unsure of the problem. Use process of elimination to get rid of unlikely answer choices whenever you can.

Number Sense and Numeration

Don't worry about big words like *numeration*. These questions deal with basic math concepts. Some of these concepts include: number lines, putting numbers in order from least to greatest, and knowing how to write numbers from words and other numbers (for example: 600 + 30 + 1 = 631).

Concepts of Whole Number Computation

These questions test how well you understand the basic facts about addition, subtraction, multiplication, and division.

Fractions and Decimals

In this group, you will find questions about fractions and decimals. You will compare numbers and figure out common denominators.

Patterns and Relationships

These questions test how well you recognize patterns. The patterns may be pictures or numbers. Often, you need to add or subtract to answer the number pattern questions.

Statistics and Probability

These questions usually involve a chart or graph. Spend some time learning more about different kind of charts and graphs. For instance, learning about pie charts and line graphs will help you greatly.

Geometry and Spatial Sense

Knowing basic geometric shapes like squares, triangles, and circles is important. You should be comfortable with coordinates and finding things on a graph.

Measurement

Many of these questions simply ask you to measure a figure correctly. Learn how to use both both metric and standard units. Other Measurement questions include: counting change, comparing lengths, or reading a scientific instrument correctly.

Estimation

These problems require you to round off numbers properly. Sometimes you will have to round off two, three, or more numbers and then add them together to get the answer.

Problem-Solving Strategies

There are different kinds of questions in this group. Some you've already done in the other parts of the test. Study those skills to help you here.

Mathematics—Procedures

Most of the questions in this section are plain and simple addition, subtraction, division, and multiplication problems. Remember, the key to answering these questions correctly is to write down all your work. Trying to answer these questions in your head often leads to careless errors. There's no reason you should waste points that way.

There are five possible answer choices on this section, not four as in the other parts of the test. The fifth choice is always NH, which stands for Not Here. If you work a problem and then do not find the answer in the first four choices, rework the problem. If you get the same answer the second time, pick NH and move on to the next question.

Rounding

These questions are like the Estimation questions in the Math—Problem Solving section. Practice rounding off numbers to the nearest tenth, hundredth, and thousandth whenever you can.

Computation in Context

These questions are mostly word problems. The key is to read the text carefully, and then decide what math operation—addition, subtraction, multiplication, or division—needs to be done to get the correct answer.

Language

Most students don't like grammar much, and that's mainly what this section tests. The problems ask you to spot errors in punctuation, capitalization, and word usage. Just remember that this is a multiple-choice test. A perfect knowledge of grammar is not needed. You just need to be able to spot incorrect grammar when you see it.

Each question in this section has four choices, and the fourth answer on the first 28 questions is always "*Correct as is.*" If you look at a question and can find no error, reread the question carefully. If you still don't find an error, simply pick *Correct as is* and move on.

Capitalization, Punctuation, and Usage

These questions each have an underlined phrase that may or may not have errors in capitalization, punctuation, and usage. If you spot the error, try to think of the way the right answer would look. For example, if you see that a word needs to be capitalized and it isn't, imagine what the correct answer should look like. Then, look down at the answer choices and pick the choice that fits your idea.

Sentence Structure

These questions include boxed-in sentences that sometimes have errors. These errors are often incomplete sentences called sentence fragments. Sometimes, there are errors in punctuation. Look at the boxed-in sentence. Can you spot an error? If so, try to imagine what the correct answer should look like. Then, look at the answer choices and find the choice that matches your idea.

Content and Organization

These questions are like Reading Comprehension questions; you will read passages and then answer questions about the text. Remember to read the passage to understand the main point, and then go back often as you do the questions.

Study Skills

This category tests your knowledge of reference materials. Reference materials include books like dictionaries and encyclopedias. There are also several problems concerning proper alphabetizing. If you need more work in this area, think of a topic that interests you, and then go to your local library and research it. Ask the librarian for help with the different reference books you use. This should help you learn more about the topics covered in these questions.

Spelling

Each of the thirty spelling questions has four answer choices. In the first three answer choices, one of the words in each sentence will be underlined. If you believe that any of the underlined words is incorrectly spelled, that choice is the answer for that question. If you look over the first three choices and believe all the words are spelled correctly, then you must pick the fourth choice, which is always *No mistake*.

Having a large vocabulary is the best key to doing well on the Spelling section. However, knowing how to add suffixes (such as the *-ed* at the end of *walked*) is also an important skill, as many spelling errors are due to incorrect suffixes. Knowing how to add *-ing* (*ride*, *riding*) and how to pluralize (*blush*, *blushes*) is a big part of that.

Ready . . . Set . . . Go!

Now you've learned some skills that will help you on the second test, and on the Stanford 9 on test day. Feel free to go over them as often as you want before you go on to take the second test. You've also discovered what subjects you're good at, and what subjects you may need some more work in. Ask your parents, teacher, or friends for help in these areas. Just remember: these tests are just practice, and you are doing well by practicing and studying. Congratulations, and keep up the good work!

Practice Test B

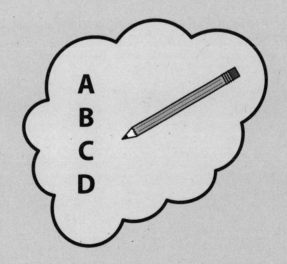

Section 1: Reading Vocabulary

20 Minutes

30 Questions

Directions: *Make sure you have a watch to time yourself and a No. 2 pencil. When you are ready, start timing yourself, and spend 20 minutes answering the questions in this section. Mark your answers on the Answer Sheet at the end of this section. If you are finished before the time is up, check over your work.*

Reading Vocabulary

Synonyms

Directions

Pick the word or phrase that means the same, or nearly the same, as the underlined word. Then mark the correct space for the answer that you have picked.

Sample

To <u>conquer</u> is to —

- Ⓐ control
- ⬤ defeat
- Ⓒ lose
- Ⓓ support

1 Something that is <u>broad</u> is —

- Ⓐ loud
- Ⓑ nice
- Ⓒ open
- Ⓓ wide

2 To <u>mend</u> something is to —

- Ⓕ burn it
- Ⓖ fix it
- Ⓗ soak it
- Ⓙ add it

3 A <u>guest</u> is a —

- Ⓐ visitor
- Ⓑ bug
- Ⓒ sign
- Ⓓ clock

4 To <u>discover</u> means to —

- Ⓕ talk
- Ⓖ aim
- Ⓗ find
- Ⓙ jump

5 To <u>combine</u> is to —

- Ⓐ know
- Ⓑ taste
- Ⓒ join
- Ⓓ pack

6 Someone who is <u>trustworthy</u> is —

- Ⓕ interesting
- Ⓖ mean
- Ⓗ honest
- Ⓙ careful

GO ON

KAPLAN

7 **Enormous** means —

Ⓐ confused
Ⓑ smart
Ⓒ big
Ⓓ old

8 To **observe** means to —

Ⓕ fight
Ⓖ watch
Ⓗ please
Ⓙ ask

9 A **master** is an —

Ⓐ expert
Ⓑ ape
Ⓒ oval
Ⓓ apple

10 **Allow** means —

Ⓕ wonder
Ⓖ freshen
Ⓗ open
Ⓙ let

11 To **examine** something is to —

Ⓐ look at it
Ⓑ throw it away
Ⓒ unwrap it
Ⓓ want it

12 A **mixture** is a —

Ⓕ size
Ⓖ book
Ⓗ store
Ⓙ blend

GO ON

13 To <u>tumble</u> is to —

(A) leap
(B) growl
(C) fall
(D) glance

14 A <u>structure</u> is a —

(F) shirt
(G) building
(H) road
(J) sign

15 Someone who is <u>hearty</u> is —

(A) sorry
(B) angry
(C) amazed
(D) healthy

16 An <u>error</u> is a —

(F) mistake
(G) story
(H) cut
(J) statement

17 To <u>march</u> is to —

(A) rain
(B) season
(C) fight
(D) walk

18 <u>Wholly</u> means —

(F) totally
(G) carelessly
(H) humorously
(J) generously

KAPLAN

Multiple Meanings

Directions

Read the sentence in each of the boxes below. Then pick the answer that uses the underlined word in the same way as the sentence in the box. Mark the correct space for the answer that you have picked.

Sample

> I will step back to let you pass.

In which sentence does the word <u>step</u> mean the same thing as in the sentence above?

- Ⓐ The third <u>step</u> on that staircase is broken.
- Ⓑ The most important <u>step</u> is to mix the batter.
- ● I will <u>step</u> on the stage.
- Ⓓ That's a <u>step</u> in the right direction.

19
> The next bus will <u>come</u> from Boston.

In which sentence does the word <u>come</u> mean the same thing as in the sentence above?

- Ⓐ I want a dress that will <u>come</u> to my knees.
- Ⓑ Don't <u>come</u> any closer.
- Ⓒ My best friend will <u>come</u> from Chicago to visit.
- Ⓓ I'll <u>come</u> to your question next.

20
> I will <u>clip</u> these papers together so I don't lose any.

In which sentence does the word <u>clip</u> mean the same thing as in the sentence above?

- Ⓕ The horse moved at a fast <u>clip</u>.
- Ⓖ She used a <u>clip</u> to hold her hair off her face.
- Ⓗ I watched a short <u>clip</u> from the movie.
- Ⓙ I will <u>clip</u> the cover of my report to the other pages.

21
> How many pages do you have <u>left</u> to read?

In which sentence does the word <u>left</u> mean the same thing as in the sentence above?

- Ⓐ I write and throw with my <u>left</u> hand.
- Ⓑ My apartment is down the hall on the <u>left</u>.
- Ⓒ Democrats are said to be on the political <u>left</u>.
- Ⓓ The were plenty of tickets <u>left</u> to buy at the game.

GO ON

22

> Take the dog for a walk around the <u>block</u>.

In which sentence does the word <u>block</u> mean the same thing as in the sentence above?

- Ⓕ The basketball player needed to <u>block</u> the shot.
- Ⓖ The baby picked up the big <u>block</u>.
- Ⓗ My best friend lives on the same <u>block</u> as me.
- Ⓙ I was upset because I had writer's <u>block</u>.

23

> My backpack was <u>light</u> when I left for school.

In which sentence does the word <u>light</u> mean the same thing as in the sentence above?

- Ⓐ The room was dark so I turned on the <u>light</u>.
- Ⓑ The suitcase was <u>light</u> before I filled it.
- Ⓒ I like only <u>light</u> sauce on my spaghetti.
- Ⓓ The sun made the room very <u>light</u>.

24

> I had to <u>run</u> to school in order not to be late.

In which sentence does the word <u>run</u> mean the same thing as in the sentence above?

- Ⓕ The baseball player scored the winning <u>run</u>.
- Ⓖ If I sleep through my alarm, I <u>run</u> late getting ready.
- Ⓗ The movie had a long <u>run</u> at the theater.
- Ⓙ Coach told me to <u>run</u> as fast as I could.

KAPLAN

Vocabulary-in-Context

Directions

When you read each of the sentences below, use the other words in the sentence to help you understand what the underlined word means. Then mark the correct space for the answer that you have picked.

Sample

She won the <u>competition</u> by beating many other fine athletes. <u>Competition</u> means —

- ⬤ contest
- Ⓑ football
- Ⓒ game
- Ⓓ run

25 I was so hungry I thought I could eat the <u>entire</u> pizza. <u>Entire</u> means —

- Ⓐ whole
- Ⓑ expensive
- Ⓒ small
- Ⓓ famous

26 He got the award in <u>recognition</u> of all his hard work. <u>Recognition</u> means —

- Ⓕ honor
- Ⓖ case
- Ⓗ pleasure
- Ⓙ direction

27 Since the earth <u>rotates</u>, different places have daylight at different times. <u>Rotates</u> means —

- Ⓐ eats
- Ⓑ stays
- Ⓒ reflects
- Ⓓ turns

28 Instead of being soft, the music was <u>blaring</u>. <u>Blaring</u> means —

- Ⓕ good
- Ⓖ loud
- Ⓗ rhythmic
- Ⓙ short

29 Even though we started in the morning, we didn't reach the <u>peak</u> of the mountain until dinner time. <u>Peak</u> means —

- Ⓐ forest
- Ⓑ valley
- Ⓒ top
- Ⓓ base

30 Over time, species of animals <u>adapt</u> to fit their habitats. <u>Adapt</u> means —

- Ⓕ change
- Ⓖ grow
- Ⓗ move
- Ⓙ return

STOP

Answer Sheet

1	(A)	(B)	(C)	(D)
2	(F)	(G)	(H)	(J)
3	(A)	(B)	(C)	(D)
4	(F)	(G)	(H)	(J)
5	(A)	(B)	(C)	(D)
6	(F)	(G)	(H)	(J)
7	(A)	(B)	(C)	(D)
8	(F)	(G)	(H)	(J)
9	(A)	(B)	(C)	(D)
10	(F)	(G)	(H)	(J)
11	(A)	(B)	(C)	(D)
12	(F)	(G)	(H)	(J)
13	(A)	(B)	(C)	(D)
14	(F)	(G)	(H)	(J)
15	(A)	(B)	(C)	(D)

16	(F)	(G)	(H)	(J)
17	(A)	(B)	(C)	(D)
18	(F)	(G)	(H)	(J)
19	(A)	(B)	(C)	(D)
20	(F)	(G)	(H)	(J)
21	(A)	(B)	(C)	(D)
22	(F)	(G)	(H)	(J)
23	(A)	(B)	(C)	(D)
24	(F)	(G)	(H)	(J)
25	(A)	(B)	(C)	(D)
26	(F)	(G)	(H)	(J)
27	(A)	(B)	(C)	(D)
28	(F)	(G)	(H)	(J)
29	(A)	(B)	(C)	(D)
30	(F)	(G)	(H)	(J)

Section 2: Reading Comprehension

50 Minutes

54 Questions

Directions: *Make sure you have a watch to time yourself and a No. 2 pencil. When you are ready, start timing yourself, and spend 50 minutes answering the questions in this section. Mark your answers on the Answer Sheet at the end of this section. If you are finished before the time is up, check over your work.*

Reading Comprehension

Directions

In this section, read the passages. Then pick the best answer for the questions that follow.

Sample

When Margarita heard the weather report predict a severe thunderstorm within the half hour, she began to worry how her younger brother would get home from his friend's house. Certainly he couldn't walk all those blocks in the rain.

Margarita's brother was —

Ⓐ doing his homework in his room
● at a friend's house
Ⓒ playing in the backyard
Ⓓ still at school

Meet the Woolly Mammoth

The woolly mammoth lived during the Ice Age. The Ice Age lasted almost 200,000 years. Scientists found fossils of the woolly mammoth. They thought the woolly mammoth was one of the earliest kinds of elephants. They even gave it a scientific name that meant "firstborn elephant." But the scientists were wrong. There were lots of kinds of elephants that lived before woolly mammoths. The first real elephants lived millions of years before the woolly mammoth. The woolly mammoth was about 10 feet tall, but the first elephants were small. They looked like pigs!

The woolly mammoth died out when the Ice Age ended. Scientists now know much more about the woolly mammoth than about most other extinct creatures. Whole mammoths were trapped and preserved in the ice. Scientists could study things like skin, hair, and tusks. The mammoth had thick hair to stay warm in the very cold weather. They ate plants that were able to grow during the Ice Age.

KAPLAN

There are many different ideas about why the woolly mammoth became extinct. It may have been hard for the mammoth to live when the ice melted and the earth got warmer. Or when humans came to be, they may have hunted and killed the woolly mammoth. Humans might have taken over the land where the woolly mammoth lived. People may have farmed where woolly mammoths used to eat.

Extinct animals are interesting to study. When you can see how they are related to animals of today, you see all the things that an animal needs to survive.

1 When did the woolly mammoth become extinct?

  Ⓐ When they grew to be 10 feet tall
  Ⓑ When dinosaurs appeared
  Ⓒ At the end of the Ice Age
  Ⓓ Before the Ice Age

2 What did the woolly mammoth's scientific name mean?

  Ⓕ "Ice Age elephant"
  Ⓖ "Firstborn elephant"
  Ⓗ "Furry elephant"
  Ⓙ "Big pig"

3 What question does the third paragraph answer?

  Ⓐ What did the woolly mammoths eat?
  Ⓑ What did the woolly mammoths look like?
  Ⓒ Why did the woolly mammoth become extinct?
  Ⓓ How was the woolly mammoth discovered?

4 How do scientists know so much about the woolly mammoth?

  Ⓕ Woolly mammoths were preserved in ice.
  Ⓖ Other kinds of elephants came before the mammoth.
  Ⓗ There are woolly mammoths still living.
  Ⓙ Books have been written on the woolly mammoth.

5 There is enough information to know that the first elephants —

  Ⓐ were hairy
  Ⓑ looked like pigs
  Ⓒ ate plants
  Ⓓ were friends with dinosaurs

GO ON

Grandfather's Stamps

Zachary's grandfather collected stamps. There were many different kinds of stamps in grandfather's collection. Some were very old, and others were very new. Some were from the United States, but others were from far away countries like China, Mexico, and France. Zachary admired Grandfather's stamps every chance he could get.

Zachary's favorite stamp was from India. Grandfather bought the stamp many years ago. It was red and blue. It had many nice shapes on it. In the center of the stamp was a young boy. Grandfather told Zachary that the young boy was a prince.

Zachary often thought about the stamp from India. He imagined that he was the prince on the stamp. In one make-believe story, Zachary pretended that he was riding a camel in the desert. He had to deliver a message to the king. Then the camel got tired. Zachary picked up the camel and carried it over the hot sand. Zachary knew that the story was not true. He liked to imagine that he was the prince anyway.

Zachary told grandfather the story about the prince in the desert. Grandfather laughed. He said to Zachary, "That is the same reason I like stamps. I like to think about the people and things on the stamps. I pretend that I know them." Zachary was happy that he and grandfather felt the same way about stamps.

GO ON

6 This story was written mainly in order to —

 Ⓕ describe a very old stamp with a prince on it

 Ⓖ tell you about a dream with a camel in the desert

 Ⓗ tell you about a boy and his grandfather's stamps

 Ⓙ give you instructions on how to collect stamps

7 Grandfather and Zachary both felt the same way about stamps because they —

 Ⓐ liked to think about the people on the stamps

 Ⓑ enjoyed looking at the many colors and shapes

 Ⓒ wished that they lived in a far away place

 Ⓓ thought that the stamps were worth a lot of money

8 Which question does the second paragraph answer?

 Ⓕ What is grandfather's favorite stamp?

 Ⓖ Where does Zachary live?

 Ⓗ What is Zachary's favorite stamp?

 Ⓙ Does Zachary's father collect stamps?

9 What is another good name for this story?

 Ⓐ "Camel in the Desert"

 Ⓑ "The Camel's Stamp"

 Ⓒ "A Stamp Story"

 Ⓓ "Zachary, the Prince"

10 Zachary pretended to carry the camel across the sand because —

 Ⓕ the camel was tired

 Ⓖ the prince did not like the camel

 Ⓗ the stamp was from India

 Ⓙ grandfather told him to

GO ON

Theater Games

Here are two popular games from acting classes. Try them at your next birthday party or during recess at school.

Game:

"Machine"

Set Up:

Everyone playing stands in a big circle.

Game Play:

The person who starts has to make a big noise and a big motion that a machine might make. Everyone has to keep making the noise and action when the next person goes. By the time it's the last person's turn, everyone is doing weird things and making loud noises!

Game:

"Telephone"

Set Up:

Everyone sits or stands in a line close together. After each round, the person who was at the front moves to the back.

Game Play:

The first person in line thinks of a funny phrase or sentence and whispers it to the next person. That person whispers it to the next person, and so on. No one says it out loud. You don't want anyone else to hear. The last person in line says what they have heard out loud. The phrase at the end will be very different from the phrase that started the game!

GO ON

11 What is the setup for "Telephone"?

    Ⓐ In a circle
    Ⓑ In a line
    Ⓒ At your desks
    Ⓓ By the phone

12 This passage is a —

    Ⓕ functional passage
    Ⓖ fiction passage
    Ⓗ nonfiction passage
    Ⓙ biography

13 In "Machine" you have to make a loud noise and —

    Ⓐ a motion
    Ⓑ a sound
    Ⓒ an excuse
    Ⓓ a story

14 In "Telephone," what happens at the end of each round?

    Ⓕ People make a big noise
    Ⓖ The person in front moves to the back
    Ⓗ A funny phrase is written down
    Ⓙ Everyone stands in a circle

15 In the passage, "make a big noise" tells you —

    Ⓐ the title of a game
    Ⓑ how to play a game
    Ⓒ how to set up a game
    Ⓓ what to do at a birthday party

GO ON

The House on the Nickel

If you look at one side of a nickel, you will see a building. If you look at the other side of the nickel, you will see Thomas Jefferson. Jefferson was the third president of the United States and the author of the Declaration of Independence. The building is the house he created for himself.

The name of the house is Monticello. This name means "little mountain." Jefferson built Monticello on top of a small mountain in Virginia. The mountain rises 580 feet above the Rivanna River. In Jefferson's time, most buildings were located near water or in valleys so that it was easy to travel. But Jefferson loved the idea of having his house on the top of a mountain.

When Jefferson planned Monticello, he acted as his own architect. He had seen many famous buildings and used ideas from those buildings to create Monticello. He included a dome, skylights, and many unusual features.

Monticello was more than a beautiful home. It was also a working farm. Jefferson grew 250 varieties of vegetables and 170 varieties of fruits. Jefferson kept careful records of how well the different foods grew.

Today Monticello is open to the public every day of the year except Christmas. Thousands of people tour the house and the gardens every year. Thousands more visit the Monticello website at www.monticello.org. If you can't visit Monticello in person or on the Web, just take a close look at a nickel.

16 **What coin has Monticello on it?**

    Ⓕ A dime

    Ⓖ A nickel

    Ⓗ A quarter

    Ⓙ A dollar

17 **Where was Monticello built?**

    Ⓐ In a valley

    Ⓑ On top of a mountain

    Ⓒ In a city

    Ⓓ Beside a farm

18 **When is Monticello open?**

    Ⓕ At Christmas

    Ⓖ All year round

    Ⓗ During the summer

    Ⓙ Every day except Christmas

GO ON

Fish Out of Water

As you know, fish live in the water. However, there is one fish, called the flying fish, that sometimes leaps above the waves. Here is a story about how the flying fish came to be.

Little Fish was sad. Every time Little Fish looked up at the surface of the ocean, she saw many different colors.

Little Fish said to Big Fish, "Can I go up above the surface of the ocean? I see many nice colors. I want to know what is there."

Big Fish frowned at Little Fish. Big Fish said, "No, Little Fish, you cannot go above the surface of the ocean. Fish like us were meant to swim in the water." Little Fish was sad and swam away to Seashell.

"Excuse me," said Little Fish to Seashell, "I would like to know what is above the surface of the ocean. Have you ever been there?"

Seashell laughed. "Of course not! I cannot go above the surface of the ocean and neither can you." Still laughing, Seashell rolled away across the bottom of the ocean.

Little Fish said to herself, "I wish I could see those beautiful colors above the surface of the ocean. Maybe Coral Reef has been up there."

Coral Reef scolded Little Fish. "How dare you, Little Fish! Things in the ocean such as fish, coral reefs, and seashells belong in the water. I think you should ignore those colors above the surface of the ocean."

Little Fish did not know what to do. Everyone told her to stay away from the surface of the ocean, but she wanted to see the nice colors.

Suddenly, Shark appeared before Little Fish. Little Fish was scared, but she knew Shark was very wise. Little Fish said, "Please, Shark, do not eat me. Tell me about what is above the surface of the ocean."

Shark thought for a moment and then said, "I do not know what is above the surface of the ocean. Like you, I have seen the beautiful colors, but I am too scared to go up there."

Little Fish made a decision. She swam quickly towards the surface of the ocean. Then Little Fish burst from the water into the air. She saw the blue sky, the yellow sun, and the brown boats. Now Little Fish was happy.

From that day on, Little Fish became known as Flying Fish. The rest of the ocean creatures learned to respect her.

19 Little fish wanted to go above the surface of the ocean because she —

   Ⓐ was scared of Shark
   Ⓑ was interested in the colors
   Ⓒ wanted to learn how to fly
   Ⓓ was tired of the ocean

20 Why was Little Fish scared of Shark?

   Ⓕ Shark knew how to fly.
   Ⓖ Shark hid behind Coral Reef.
   Ⓗ Shark had been above the surface.
   Ⓙ Shark could eat Little Fish.

21 This story was written to tell —

   Ⓐ how the flying fish got its name
   Ⓑ why sharks eat other fish
   Ⓒ how boats float on the water
   Ⓓ why fish live in the ocean

22 You can tell this story is make-believe because —

   Ⓕ sharks do not eat little fish
   Ⓖ you cannot see colors under water
   Ⓗ coral reefs do not appear in the ocean
   Ⓙ fish cannot talk

23 The boxes show some things that happened in the story.

1

| Big Fish frowned at Little Fish. |

2

| |

3

| Coral Reef scolded Little Fish. |

Which of these belongs in Box 2?

   Ⓐ Little Fish flew above the water.
   Ⓑ Shark warned Little Fish.
   Ⓒ Seashell laughed at Little Fish.
   Ⓓ Little Fish was named Flying Fish.

 GO ON

Scratch Goes to School

Anna had no idea how she was going to figure this out. She looked at her watch again. It was ten minutes before she was supposed to be at her babysitter's house. She had a good view of her classroom door from where she was standing. She would see as soon as anyone came out. But no one was coming out, and Anna had to get in. Her kitten was in there!

Scratch had followed Anna to school that morning. Now Anna was in trouble because her teacher was having a meeting in the classroom with a bunch of parents. There was no way Anna could get in the classroom!

Anna looked at her watch. No one had come out of the door. If Anna didn't get Scratch, she was going to be late to her babysitter's house.

GO ON

24 Another good name for this story is —

    Ⓕ "A Cat in Class"

    Ⓖ "The Teacher"

    Ⓗ "Looking at Your Watch"

    Ⓙ "Figure This Out"

25 What kind of passage is this?

    Ⓐ A functional passage

    Ⓑ A fiction passage

    Ⓒ A nonfiction passage

    Ⓓ A science passage

26 Why did Anna keep looking at her watch?

    Ⓕ She was going to be late

    Ⓖ A friend was late

    Ⓗ She was hungry

    Ⓙ The bus was waiting

27 What was Anna going to be late for?

    Ⓐ Her cat's dinnertime

    Ⓑ A meeting with a group of parents

    Ⓒ Her last class of the day

    Ⓓ A visit to her babysitter's house

28 At the end of this story, Anna is most likely —

    Ⓕ calm

    Ⓖ happy

    Ⓗ impatient

    Ⓙ tired

GO ON

Thumb Print Cookies

This recipe combines an old-fashioned recipe with fun fillings you can pick and put in yourself!

Ingredients:

$1\frac{1}{2}$ cups flour

$\frac{1}{3}$ cup white sugar

$\frac{3}{4}$ cup butter

small bowl of ice water

jelly (any kind)

chocolate filling

Directions:

1. Preheat oven to 350 degrees (ask for help with this).

2. Blend all ingredients well.

3. Put dough in refrigerator for about an hour—or until dough is cool and stiff.

4. With clean hands, roll dough into ping-pong ball sized balls. Place on buttered cookie sheet.

5. Dip your thumb in the bowl of ice water and make a dent in the center of each cookie. Be careful that the hole **does not** go all the way through to cookie sheet.

6. Fill holes with jelly or chocolate.

7. Bake until golden brown on edges (ask for help with this).

Yield:

About 2 dozen (24 cookies)

29 When should you preheat the oven?

    Ⓐ Before you do anything else

    Ⓑ After you refrigerate the dough

    Ⓒ Before you choose your fillings

    Ⓓ After you make the dent in each cookie

30 Where will you probably mix all the ingredients?

    Ⓕ On the floor

    Ⓖ On a plate

    Ⓗ In the sink

    Ⓙ In a bowl

31 Why should you be sure the thumb print does not go all the way through?

    Ⓐ The cookies will not look good

    Ⓑ The filling will leak through

    Ⓒ The cookies will not cook

    Ⓓ The cookies will not stay the right size

32 You need the help of an adult to —

    Ⓕ make a bowl of ice water

    Ⓖ roll the dough into balls

    Ⓗ work with the oven

    Ⓙ mix the ingredients

GO ON

ANNUAL SCHOOL FOOD FESTIVAL

Enjoy great food from around the world!

The French Club presents French cheese and bread.

10 A.M.–11:30 A.M. in the cafeteria

Come taste this delicious food and see pictures of the French countryside.

See Ms. Bartolo for more information.

Mexican Treats!

Tacos, burritos, and enchiladas—11 A.M.–12:00 P.M.

Mexican desserts—12:30 P.M–1:30 P.M.

Room 332

Sponsored by Taco Hut on West Main St. 555-9856

Cakes! Cakes! Cakes!

The Cooking Club will present a variety of cakes for you to sample.

10 A.M.–12:00 P.M. in the Home Economics Room

Enter the recipe contest. The winner will get a free baking dish.

Speak with Mr. Martin for a contest entry form.

A Sushi Party

The Tikito Restaurant will bring in a variety of sushi.

Taste fresh raw fish wrapped in seaweed and rice.

12:00 P.M.–2:00 P.M. in the cafeteria

The Tikito Restaurant is located on South Street. 555-9078

GO ON

33 Who should you see if you want a contest entry form?

- Ⓐ The Tikito Restaurant
- Ⓑ Taco Hut
- Ⓒ Mr. Martin
- Ⓓ Ms. Bartolo

34 Where will the French Club hold its presentation?

- Ⓕ The cafeteria
- Ⓖ The Home Economics Room
- Ⓗ Room 332
- Ⓙ The notice does not say.

35 Which food can someone try in Room 332?

- Ⓐ Sushi
- Ⓑ Mexican food
- Ⓒ French food
- Ⓓ Cakes

36 Which food is <u>not</u> mentioned in the notices?

- Ⓕ Tacos
- Ⓖ Cakes
- Ⓗ Fruit
- Ⓙ Sushi

37 What will the winner of the recipe contest get?

- Ⓐ A baking dish
- Ⓑ Free food
- Ⓒ A surprise gift
- Ⓓ A recipe book

Ceramics on the Wheel

Lots of vases and bowls that you see in stores are made from clay. Artists "throw" the clay on a potter's wheel and give it the shape you see. The potter's wheel is not like a car wheel. It's like a big round plate that spins around and around. You shape the clay as the wheel spins. Building ceramics on a wheel is a hard and long process.

The first thing you have to do is make sure the clay is ready to be thrown. You have to knead it like you knead dough. You have to make sure there are no air bubbles left. Air bubbles in the clay can pop and crack the piece as you are building it. The clay can also crack as it's drying.

Once the clay is ready, you have to make it into the shape of an egg. It is important that the piece is shaped nicely. The shape lets you make what you want. The egg turns into a vase or bowl.

The third step is to "center" the egg in the middle of the pottery wheel. Some people think that centering is the hardest thing to do. You have to do it perfectly if you want to have a good result at the end of the project. Once you have "thrown" the clay onto the center of the wheel, you're ready to start! Make sure you have water, a sponge, and lots of patience.

GO ON

38 Which is probably made from clay thrown on a wheel?

    Ⓕ A plate

    Ⓖ A vase

    Ⓗ A bed

    Ⓙ A spoon

39 When you throw the clay onto the wheel, it should look like —

    Ⓐ a wheel

    Ⓑ a triangle

    Ⓒ a perfect circle

    Ⓓ an egg

40 Which question does the third paragraph answer?

    Ⓕ Why does the clay have to be shaped like an egg?

    Ⓖ What are the steps to kneading clay?

    Ⓗ Why is it important to have water nearby?

    Ⓙ When can air bubbles harm the clay?

41 To find out more about using the pottery wheel, you should —

    Ⓐ look up the word "pottery" in the dictionary

    Ⓑ ask a painter

    Ⓒ visit an art museum

    Ⓓ read a book about working with clay

42 Another title for this passage is —

    Ⓕ "Getting Ready to Use a Pottery Wheel"

    Ⓖ "Having Fun with Art"

    Ⓗ "How to Build a Vase"

    Ⓙ "Painting Clay"

GO ON

Tennis

For some people, tennis is the most exciting game in the world. It is very easy to learn, and people of all ages can play. People around the world enjoy both watching and playing tennis.

Most tennis matches are played by two people, one against the other. The two people stand on opposite ends of a rectangular playing area known as a court. There is a net between the two players. The net is about two feet high and runs across the width of the court, separating the two players from each other.

Each player has a tennis racket. Like a small broom, a tennis racket has a handle the player holds in his hand. The other end of the racket is an open circle, but inside the circle are a series of strings forming a tight net, like a spider's web. The players use the webbed part of their racket to hit a tennis ball to each other across the net. A tennis ball is a small, fuzzy ball about 10 inches around and filled with air.

In a tennis match, one player starts the action by hitting the ball to the other player. The players then take turns and **volley** the ball back and forth over the net until someone wins the point. A player wins the point if his opponent hits the ball outside the court, or out of bounds. A player can also win the point if he hits the ball to his opponent and his opponent is unable to hit the ball back across the net. Also, the ball is allowed to bounce only one time on each side of the court. If a player is unable to hit the ball before it bounces twice, he loses the point.

Tennis can also be played as a game for four people. When four people play, two people stand on each side of the net. These players are on the same team, and they try to win points off the players on the other team. This type of tennis has almost the same set of rules as when only two people play tennis. So if one of the tennis teams hits the ball outside of the tennis court, the other team wins the point.

Some people who play tennis are so good at the sport that they make a living just playing tennis. Whenever two of these **brilliant** players have a tennis match against each other, thousands of people travel for many miles just to watch. Many more watch the event on television, as these matches show some of the best tennis in the world. Yet even if a person is not a good tennis player, a game of tennis is still a good way to spend an afternoon with a friend.

GO ON

43 In this story, the word *volley* means —

   Ⓐ catch the ball with your hands

   Ⓑ hold the ball with your racket

   Ⓒ hit the ball with your racket

   Ⓓ bounce the ball with your hands

44 The word *brilliant* in this story means —

   Ⓕ very good

   Ⓖ ordinary

   Ⓗ long

   Ⓙ speedy

45 Tennis can be played by —

   Ⓐ two people only

   Ⓑ four people only

   Ⓒ children only

   Ⓓ anyone

46 How do most tennis fans probably feel when they attend a tennis match?

   Ⓕ worried

   Ⓖ excited

   Ⓗ brave

   Ⓙ tired

47 This story is mostly about —

   Ⓐ when tennis is played

   Ⓑ when to hit the tennis ball

   Ⓒ how tennis is played

   Ⓓ why people watch tennis

GO ON

The Third-Grade Talent Show

Laura Zegman was looking forward to seeing her younger brothers' talent show. It was the first talent show ever for the twins, and they had worked on their juggling act to prepare for this evening.

It was about time for the talent show to start. Laura's father handed her a piece of paper as she sat down next to her parents. "It's a schedule of the talent show."

Brazelton Elementary School Presents

The Third Annual Third-Grade Talent Show
Thursday, March 23, at 6:30 in the Gym
Fruit and punch will be served in the cafeteria after the show.

Schedule of Acts

6:30	Introduction	Principal Ertel Hall
6:45	Song, "We Are the World"	Jacqueline Biedenfeld
6:50	Ballet, "Swan Lake"	Pete Szcerbiak
7:00	The Juggling Zegmans	Ernst and Mike Zegman
7:10	Piano, "21st Century Chopsticks"	Portia Heimdall
7:30	Magic Act, "The Vanishing Snail"	Walter Ross
7:40	Song, "Camptown Races"	Joanie Iber
7:55	Closing Remarks	Principal Ertel Hall
8:00	End of Talent Show	

The talent show performers would like to thank the following people for their help in making this show possible:

Ms. Claudia Baba for helping set up the stage.

Ms. Alexis Biedenfeld for loaning her favorite snail for the Magic Act.

Mr. Mark Kossover for helping with the lighting.

All our families for giving us their support.

GO ON

48 How did Laura feel about going to the talent show?

- Ⓕ scared
- Ⓖ puzzled
- Ⓗ interested
- Ⓙ disappointed

49 If the schedule is correct, which act will probably take longer than any other?

- Ⓐ the juggling
- Ⓑ the singing
- Ⓒ the ballet dancing
- Ⓓ the piano playing

50 What will happen just after the talent show ends?

- Ⓕ Fruit will be served.
- Ⓖ Schedules will be handed out.
- Ⓗ The stage will be set up.
- Ⓙ The principal will make an introduction.

51 Why did Laura attend the talent show?

- Ⓐ She wanted to see the magic act.
- Ⓑ She wanted to see the juggling act.
- Ⓒ She likes fruit and punch.
- Ⓓ Her parents made her attend.

52 Alexis Biedenfeld helped with the talent show by —

- Ⓕ loaning her snail
- Ⓖ singing the song "We Are the World"
- Ⓗ helping set up the stage
- Ⓙ serving punch in the cafeteria

53 This story is mostly about how Laura —

- Ⓐ sat down next to her mother and father
- Ⓑ liked to watch juggling at the talent show
- Ⓒ helped her brothers practice their act
- Ⓓ learned about the acts in the talent show

54 How many nonsinging acts does the Talent Show have?

- Ⓕ 9
- Ⓖ 7
- Ⓗ 6
- Ⓙ 4

STOP

Answer Sheet

1	A	B	C	D
2	F	G	H	J
3	A	B	C	D
4	F	G	H	J
5	A	B	C	D
6	F	G	H	J
7	A	B	C	D
8	F	G	H	J
9	A	B	C	D
10	F	G	H	J
11	A	B	C	D
12	F	G	H	J
13	A	B	C	D
14	F	G	H	J
15	A	B	C	D
16	F	G	H	J
17	A	B	C	D
18	F	G	H	J
19	A	B	C	D
20	F	G	H	J
21	A	B	C	D
22	F	G	H	J
23	A	B	C	D
24	F	G	H	J
25	A	B	C	D
26	F	G	H	J
27	A	B	C	D

28	F	G	H	J
29	A	B	C	D
30	F	G	H	J
31	A	B	C	D
32	F	G	H	J
33	A	B	C	D
34	F	G	H	J
35	A	B	C	D
36	F	G	H	J
37	A	B	C	D
38	F	G	H	J
39	A	B	C	D
40	F	G	H	J
41	A	B	C	D
42	F	G	H	J
43	A	B	C	D
44	F	G	H	J
45	A	B	C	D
46	F	G	H	J
47	A	B	C	D
48	F	G	H	J
49	A	B	C	D
50	F	G	H	J
51	A	B	C	D
52	F	G	H	J
53	A	B	C	D
54	F	G	H	J

Section 3: Mathematics— Problem Solving

50 Minutes

46 Questions

Directions: *Make sure you have a watch to time yourself, a No. 2 pencil, and a ruler that has both metric and standard units. When you are ready, start timing yourself, and spend 50 minutes answering the questions in this section. Mark your answers on the Answer Sheet at the end of this section. If you are finished before the time is up, check over your work.*

Mathematics— Problem Solving

Directions

Read each question. Choose the best answer and mark that space.

Sample

Maria developed 24 pictures of her birthday party and 36 pictures of her sister's wedding. How many pictures did she develop all together?

Ⓐ 50

Ⓑ 59

⬤ 60

Ⓓ 100

1 What number means 7,000 + 500 + 8?

Ⓐ 758

Ⓑ 7,508

Ⓒ 75,008

Ⓓ 750,008

2 A company sold these cars last year.

Color	Cars Sold
Red	543
Blue	362
Black	598
White	450

Which lists the cars from the color sold most to the color sold least?

Ⓕ Blue, White, Red, Black

Ⓖ White, Blue, Red, Black

Ⓗ Black, Red, White, Blue

Ⓙ Blue, White, Black, Red

3 April picked 1,390 apples last year. What is the value of the 3 in 1,390?

Ⓐ three thousand

Ⓑ three hundred

Ⓒ thirty

Ⓓ three

GO ON

4 Which bag of potato chips has the lowest cost per chip?

Bag	Cost per Chip
Ridges	2.1¢
Chippos	2.4¢
Snackets	1.7¢
Tateroos	2.8¢

Ⓕ Ridges

Ⓖ Chippos

Ⓗ Snackets

Ⓙ Tateroos

5 Four stores had sales on jeans. Which store sold the most jeans?

Store	Number Sold
Clothes King	567
Jeans City	625
Dress Store	582
Pricey Pants	63

Ⓐ Clothes King

Ⓑ Jeans City

Ⓒ Dress Store

Ⓓ Pricey Pants

6 The library has ordered two thousand five hundred sixty-two books since it opened. Which shows that number?

Ⓕ 256

Ⓖ 2,562

Ⓗ 25,562

Ⓙ 250,062

7 Which number sentence is in the same family of facts as $2 + 7 = 9$?

Ⓐ $9 - 7 = 2$

Ⓑ $2 + 9 = 11$

Ⓒ $7 + 9 = 16$

Ⓓ $2 \times 7 = 14$

8 Jeff sold 50 newspapers on Thursday. He sold 35 newspapers on Friday. Which number sentence could you use to figure out how many newspapers he sold all together both days?

Ⓕ $50 + 35 = \square$

Ⓖ $50 - 35 = \square$

Ⓗ $50 \times 35 = \square$

Ⓙ $50 \div 35 = \square$

GO ON

9 Beth runs every day for 40 minutes. She has already run for 25 minutes today. Which number sentence could you use to figure out how many more minutes she will run today?

Ⓐ $40 + 25 = \square$

Ⓑ $40 - 25 = \square$

Ⓒ $40 \times 25 = \square$

Ⓓ $40 \div 25 = \square$

10 Jean earns $20 per week babysitting. She has already earned $12 this week. Which number sentence could you use to find out how much more she will earn this week?

Ⓕ $\$20 - \$12 = \square$

Ⓖ $\$20 + \$12 = \square$

Ⓗ $\$20 \times \square = \$12$

Ⓙ $\$20 \div \square = \$12$

11 Mr. Joseph brought a jar of hot fudge home after work so he could make sundaes with his family. At the end of the night, the jar was $\frac{1}{2}$ full. Which could be the jar after the family made sundaes?

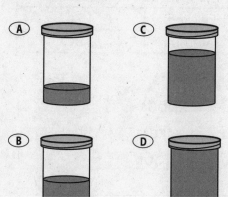

GO ON

KAPLAN

12 Timmy went apple picking with his family one weekend. In order to pay the orchard, they had to separate the apples by type. They made up this chart.

Type of Apple	Fraction of All Apples Picked
Red Delicious	$\frac{1}{4}$
Granny Smith	$\frac{1}{2}$
Macoun	$\frac{1}{6}$
Golden Delicious	$\frac{1}{12}$

What type of apple did Timmy's family take home the most of?

Ⓕ Red Delicious

Ⓖ Granny Smith

Ⓗ Macoun

Ⓙ Golden Delicious

13 Danielle bought pretzels and popcorn for her friends at the baseball game. $\frac{1}{3}$ of what she bought was pretzels and $\frac{2}{3}$ was popcorn. Which could be what Danielle bought?

Ⓐ

Ⓑ

Ⓒ

Ⓓ

14 What fraction of the square is shaded?

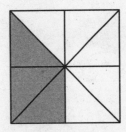

Ⓕ $\frac{1}{6}$

Ⓖ $\frac{3}{8}$

Ⓗ $\frac{5}{8}$

Ⓙ $\frac{8}{9}$

GO ON

15 Rick takes the painting of his house below and turns it upside down.

Which picture shows the painting turned upside down?

Ⓐ

Ⓒ

Ⓑ

Ⓓ

16 Four types of beans are poured on a table. If a bean is chosen at random, which type is the least likely to be chosen?

Ⓕ

Ⓗ

Ⓖ

Ⓙ

17 Look at the number pattern below:

13, 9, 5, _____

What number will be next in the pattern?

Ⓐ 0

Ⓑ 1

Ⓒ 3

Ⓓ 4

GO ON

KAPLAN

Ms. Kay keeps a tally chart of how many students answer each question on a test correctly. Use the chart to answer questions 18 and 19.

Question Number	Students Answering Correctly
1	⁄⁄⁄⁄ ⁄⁄⁄⁄ ⁄⁄⁄⁄ ⁄⁄⁄⁄ |||
2	⁄⁄⁄⁄ ⁄⁄⁄⁄ ⁄⁄⁄⁄ |||
3	⁄⁄⁄⁄ ⁄⁄⁄⁄ ⁄⁄⁄⁄ ⁄⁄⁄⁄ ||
4	⁄⁄⁄⁄ ⁄⁄⁄⁄ ⁄⁄⁄⁄ ||
5	⁄⁄⁄⁄ |||

18 Which question did the most students answer correctly?

(F) Question 1

(G) Question 2

(H) Question 3

(J) Question 4

19 If Sam answered 4 questions correctly, which question did he most likely answer wrong?

(A) Question 1

(B) Question 3

(C) Question 4

(D) Question 5

Harry runs every day. The number of miles he ran on four different days last week is shown in the bar graph below. Use the graph to answer questions 20 and 21.

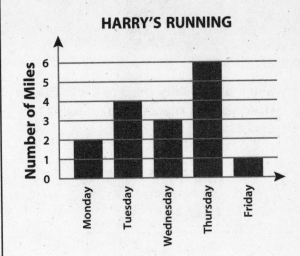

HARRY'S RUNNING

20 On which day did Harry run 6 miles?

(F) Monday

(G) Tuesday

(H) Wednesday

(J) Thursday

21 On which day did Harry run 2 more miles than he did on Friday?

(A) Monday

(B) Tuesday

(C) Wednesday

(D) Thursday

GO ON

Olivia counts the different flavors of jellybeans in a jar.

She makes a tally chart of her results. Use this tally chart for questions 22 and 23:

Jelly Beans in Jar

Flavor	Number of Jelly Beans
Cherry	̶H̶H̶H̶ II
Lemon	̶H̶H̶H̶ ̶H̶H̶H̶
Sour Apple	IIII
Blueberry	̶H̶H̶H̶ IIII
Orange	III

22 How many blueberry jellybeans are in the jar?

- Ⓕ 14
- Ⓖ 10
- Ⓗ 9
- Ⓙ 6

23 Which flavor has the most jellybeans in the jar?

- Ⓐ Cherry
- Ⓑ Lemon
- Ⓒ Blueberry
- Ⓓ Orange

24 Which of these are the same shape and size?

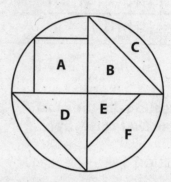

- Ⓕ A and B
- Ⓖ B and D
- Ⓗ D and E
- Ⓙ C and F

GO ON

25 Which shape has only four corners and is shaded?

26 Which has a front shaped like a triangle?

27 You are looking for a number inside the circle. It is also inside the triangle. It is NOT inside the square. What number are you looking for?

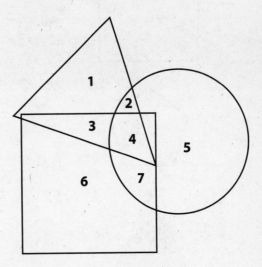

- Ⓐ 1
- Ⓑ 2
- Ⓒ 4
- Ⓓ 5

GO ON

28 Which shape has only four corners and is NOT shaded?

Ⓕ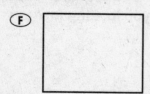

Ⓖ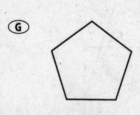

Ⓗ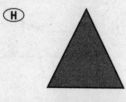

Ⓙ

29 Which has a top with a circle shape?

Ⓐ

Ⓑ

Ⓒ

Ⓓ

30 Use your inch ruler to measure this leaf. How long is this leaf?

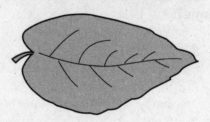

Ⓕ 4 inches

Ⓖ 3 inches

Ⓗ 2 inches

Ⓙ 1 inch

GO ON

31 Alice has a fish tank at home. Which units would she use to measure how much water it holds?

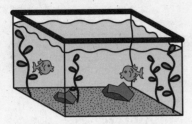

- Ⓐ Gallons
- Ⓑ Inches
- Ⓒ Feet
- Ⓓ Pounds

32 Use your centimeter ruler to measure the path from the toy car to the race track.

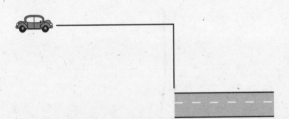

- Ⓕ 8 centimeters
- Ⓖ 7 centimeters
- Ⓗ 6 centimeters
- Ⓙ 5 centimeters

33 Chris has one quarter, one dime, and one penny in her pocket.

What is the total value of her coins?

- Ⓐ 36¢
- Ⓑ 35¢
- Ⓒ 26¢
- Ⓓ 25¢

34 Mr. Lorry caught a fish off the pier. Which units would he use to measure the length of the fish he caught?

- Ⓕ Gallons
- Ⓖ Pounds
- Ⓗ Inches
- Ⓙ Quarts

GO ON

35 How many inches long is this piece of string?

   Ⓐ 6 inches

   Ⓑ 7 inches

   Ⓒ 8 inches

   Ⓓ 9 inches

36

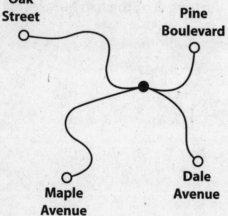

Which road on this map is the shortest?

   Ⓕ Oak Street

   Ⓖ Pine Boulevard

   Ⓗ Maple Avenue

   Ⓙ Dale Avenue

37 Use your centimeter ruler to help answer this question. How long is the hammer?

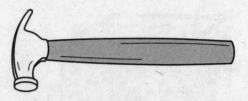

   Ⓐ 3 centimeters

   Ⓑ 6 centimeters

   Ⓒ 9 centimeters

   Ⓓ 12 centimeters

38 Use your centimeter ruler for this question. How long is this spoon?

   Ⓕ 2 centimeters

   Ⓖ 4 centimeters

   Ⓗ 5 centimeters

   Ⓙ 6 centimeters

GO ON

39 Janice and Judy played in the snow after school. Which shows the most likely temperature that day?

    (A) 30° F

    (B) 48° F

    (C) 67° F

    (D) 85° F

40 Carrie drove 128 miles to visit her grandparents. What is that number rounded to the nearer ten?

    (F) 100

    (G) 120

    (H) 130

    (J) 200

41 *About* how many students are in the school?

Class	Number of Students
Kindergarten	21
First Grade	33
Second Grade	37
Third Grade	29
Fourth Grade	39

    (A) 100

    (B) 160

    (C) 200

    (D) 260

42 Jared's reading club has 10 members. Each member read between 7 and 11 books over the summer. Which is the most reasonable estimate of the total number of books the book club read?

    (F) 60

    (G) 70

    (H) 90

    (J) 120

43 Hank left his house at 4:30 and walked to a movie theater. What else would you need to know in order to figure out what time he arrived at the movie theater?

    (A) How long he took to walk to the movie theater

    (B) Which movie he went to see

    (C) Where he lives

    (D) If he is meeting anyone there

GO ON

44 Sophie's goal is to read 45 books during the school year. If she has read 34, how many does she still need to read in order to reach her goal?

- Ⓕ 9
- Ⓖ 11
- Ⓗ 14
- Ⓙ 21

45 Sam made cookies for the bake sale at school. He put 4 cookies into each bag. If 17 bags were sold, how many cookies were sold in all?

- Ⓐ 19
- Ⓑ 64
- Ⓒ 68
- Ⓓ 74

46 Janice received two nickels and a penny as change when she bought a soda. What else do you need to know to find out how much the soda cost?

- Ⓕ The type of soda she bought
- Ⓖ How big the soda was
- Ⓗ What year the penny was made
- Ⓙ How much money she gave the clerk

STOP

Answer Sheet

1 (A) (B) (C) (D)
2 (F) (G) (H) (J)
3 (A) (B) (C) (D)
4 (F) (G) (H) (J)
5 (A) (B) (C) (D)
6 (F) (G) (H) (J)
7 (A) (B) (C) (D)
8 (F) (G) (H) (J)
9 (A) (B) (C) (D)
10 (F) (G) (H) (J)
11 (A) (B) (C) (D)
12 (F) (G) (H) (J)
13 (A) (B) (C) (D)
14 (F) (G) (H) (J)
15 (A) (B) (C) (D)
16 (F) (G) (H) (J)
17 (A) (B) (C) (D)
18 (F) (G) (H) (J)
19 (A) (B) (C) (D)
20 (F) (G) (H) (J)
21 (A) (B) (C) (D)
22 (F) (G) (H) (J)
23 (A) (B) (C) (D)

24 (F) (G) (H) (J)
25 (A) (B) (C) (D)
26 (F) (G) (H) (J)
27 (A) (B) (C) (D)
28 (F) (G) (H) (J)
29 (A) (B) (C) (D)
30 (F) (G) (H) (J)
31 (A) (B) (C) (D)
32 (F) (G) (H) (J)
33 (A) (B) (C) (D)
34 (F) (G) (H) (J)
35 (A) (B) (C) (D)
36 (F) (G) (H) (J)
37 (A) (B) (C) (D)
38 (F) (G) (H) (J)
39 (A) (B) (C) (D)
40 (F) (G) (H) (J)
41 (A) (B) (C) (D)
42 (F) (G) (H) (J)
43 (A) (B) (C) (D)
44 (F) (G) (H) (J)
45 (A) (B) (C) (D)
46 (F) (G) (H) (J)

Section 4: Mathematics— Procedures

30 Minutes

30 Questions

Directions: *Make sure you have a watch to time yourself, a No. 2 pencil, and a ruler that has both metric and standard units. When you are ready, start timing yourself, and spend 30 minutes answering the questions in this section. Mark your answers on the Answer Sheet at the end of this section. If you are finished before the time is up, check over your work.*

Mathematics— Procedures

Directions

Read each question. Choose the best answer and mark that space. If you are certain that the answer is <u>not here</u>, mark NH.

Sample

$$151 + 120$$

- Ⓐ 31
- Ⓑ 251
- Ⓒ 270
- ⬤ 271
- Ⓔ NH

1

$$629 - 357$$

- Ⓐ 372
- Ⓑ 332
- Ⓒ 272
- Ⓓ 244
- Ⓔ NH

2 $7 \times 5 = \boxed{}$

- Ⓕ 75
- Ⓖ 42
- Ⓗ 35
- Ⓙ 28
- Ⓚ NH

3

$$6 \times 8$$

- Ⓐ 48
- Ⓑ 24
- Ⓒ 16
- Ⓓ 14
- Ⓔ NH

4

$$480 \times 3$$

- Ⓕ 1540
- Ⓖ 1440
- Ⓗ 1280
- Ⓙ 1243
- Ⓚ NH

5 $17 \times 10 = \boxed{}$

- Ⓐ 170
- Ⓑ 171
- Ⓒ 270
- Ⓓ 1710
- Ⓔ NH

6 $56 \div 7 = \boxed{}$

- Ⓕ 6
- Ⓖ 7
- Ⓗ 8
- Ⓙ 9
- Ⓚ NH

GO ON

7   63
      − 36

Ⓐ 99

Ⓑ 33

Ⓒ 27

Ⓓ 23

Ⓔ NH

8   8)‾32‾

Ⓕ 3

Ⓖ 4

Ⓗ 5

Ⓙ 6

Ⓚ NH

9   528
      + 43

Ⓐ 561

Ⓑ 571

Ⓒ 601

Ⓓ 958

Ⓔ NH

10   231
      − 77

Ⓕ 154

Ⓖ 166

Ⓗ 254

Ⓙ 308

Ⓚ NH

11 $4 \times 81 =$ ☐

Ⓐ 85

Ⓑ 121

Ⓒ 324

Ⓓ 325

Ⓔ NH

12   23
      × 2

Ⓕ 25

Ⓖ 43

Ⓗ 46

Ⓙ 47

Ⓚ NH

GO ON

13

$$\begin{array}{r} 224 \\ -\ 62 \\ \hline \end{array}$$

- (A) 162
- (B) 166
- (C) 172
- (D) 242
- (E) NH

14 $6\overline{)54}$

- (F) 9
- (G) 8
- (H) 7
- (J) 6
- (K) NH

15 $7\overline{)49}$

- (A) 6
- (B) 7
- (C) 8
- (D) 9
- (E) NH

16 $24 \div 6$

- (F) 2
- (G) 5
- (H) 6
- (J) 8
- (K) NH

17 63×100

- (A) 631
- (B) 6,300
- (C) 6,310
- (D) 6,400
- (E) NH

18 $7\overline{)63}$

- (F) 441
- (G) 8
- (H) 7
- (J) 6
- (K) NH

GO ON

19 Marcy lives at 689 Hill Street. What is that number rounded to the nearer hundred?

Ⓐ 600
Ⓑ 680
Ⓒ 690
Ⓓ 700
Ⓔ NH

20 Sandy weighs 47 pounds. What is that number rounded to the nearer ten?

Ⓕ 55
Ⓖ 50
Ⓗ 45
Ⓙ 40
Ⓚ NH

21 *About* how many hot dogs were sold at the carnival?

Type of Hot Dog	Number Sold
Hot dog with ketchup	42
Hot dog with mustard	28
Hot dog with sauerkraut	18
Hot dog with relish	11

Ⓐ 60
Ⓑ 85
Ⓒ 100
Ⓓ 150
Ⓔ NH

22 Yesterday Shawn took her dog for a 15 minute walk. Today she walked her dog for 25 minutes. How many minutes all together did Shawn walk her dog those two days?

Ⓕ 50
Ⓖ 40
Ⓗ 35
Ⓙ 10
Ⓚ NH

GO ON

23 In Mrs. Abel's class, the desks are lined up in 4 rows. In each row, there are 6 students. How many students are in the class?

Ⓐ 10

Ⓑ 12

Ⓒ 24

Ⓓ 30

Ⓔ NH

24 Elana bought some groceries for $15.84.

She paid with a twenty-dollar bill.

If there was no tax, how much change should Elana receive?

Ⓕ $5.26

Ⓖ $5.16

Ⓗ $4.26

Ⓙ $4.16

Ⓚ NH

25 Courtney, Kaitlyn, and Kristin went apple picking. Courtney picked 13 apples, Kaitlyn picked 11 apples and Kristin picked 7 apples. How many apples did they pick all together?

Ⓐ 27

Ⓑ 31

Ⓒ 38

Ⓓ 41

Ⓔ NH

26 Roy has 5 bags of candy. Each bag has 7 pieces of candy in it.

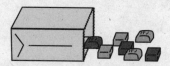

How many pieces of candy does Roy have all together?

Ⓕ 7

Ⓖ 12

Ⓗ 35

Ⓙ 45

Ⓚ NH

GO ON

27 143 light bulbs need to be replaced in a hotel. Alex replaced 77 of the light bulbs in the morning.

143

77

How many light bulbs does he have left to replace?

(A) 64

(B) 66

(C) 76

(D) 77

(E) NH

28 Ingrid paid $3.24 for a sandwich. She gave the clerk a five-dollar bill. If there was no tax, how much change should Ingrid receive?

(F) $2.76

(G) $2.24

(H) $1.86

(J) $1.76

(K) NH

29 Jerry won 5 packets of trading cards at a fair. Each packet has 8 cards. How many cards did Jerry win in all?

(A) 40

(B) 45

(C) 58

(D) 85

(E) NH

30 In a full parking lot, there were 15 rows with 6 cars parked in each row.

15

How many cars were parked in the lot?

(F) 65

(G) 90

(H) 105

(J) 156

(K) NH

STOP

Answer Sheet

1 Ⓐ Ⓑ Ⓒ Ⓓ Ⓔ
2 Ⓕ Ⓖ Ⓗ Ⓙ Ⓚ
3 Ⓐ Ⓑ Ⓒ Ⓓ Ⓔ
4 Ⓕ Ⓖ Ⓗ Ⓙ Ⓚ
5 Ⓐ Ⓑ Ⓒ Ⓓ Ⓔ
6 Ⓕ Ⓖ Ⓗ Ⓙ Ⓚ
7 Ⓐ Ⓑ Ⓒ Ⓓ Ⓔ
8 Ⓕ Ⓖ Ⓗ Ⓙ Ⓚ
9 Ⓐ Ⓑ Ⓒ Ⓓ Ⓔ
10 Ⓕ Ⓖ Ⓗ Ⓙ Ⓚ
11 Ⓐ Ⓑ Ⓒ Ⓓ Ⓔ
12 Ⓕ Ⓖ Ⓗ Ⓙ Ⓚ
13 Ⓐ Ⓑ Ⓒ Ⓓ Ⓔ
14 Ⓕ Ⓖ Ⓗ Ⓙ Ⓚ
15 Ⓐ Ⓑ Ⓒ Ⓓ Ⓔ

16 Ⓕ Ⓖ Ⓗ Ⓙ Ⓚ
17 Ⓐ Ⓑ Ⓒ Ⓓ Ⓔ
18 Ⓕ Ⓖ Ⓗ Ⓙ Ⓚ
19 Ⓐ Ⓑ Ⓒ Ⓓ Ⓔ
20 Ⓕ Ⓖ Ⓗ Ⓙ Ⓚ
21 Ⓐ Ⓑ Ⓒ Ⓓ Ⓔ
22 Ⓕ Ⓖ Ⓗ Ⓙ Ⓚ
23 Ⓐ Ⓑ Ⓒ Ⓓ Ⓔ
24 Ⓕ Ⓖ Ⓗ Ⓙ Ⓚ
25 Ⓐ Ⓑ Ⓒ Ⓓ Ⓔ
26 Ⓕ Ⓖ Ⓗ Ⓙ Ⓚ
27 Ⓐ Ⓑ Ⓒ Ⓓ Ⓔ
28 Ⓕ Ⓖ Ⓗ Ⓙ Ⓚ
29 Ⓐ Ⓑ Ⓒ Ⓓ Ⓔ
30 Ⓕ Ⓖ Ⓗ Ⓙ Ⓚ

Section 5: Language

45 Minutes

48 Questions

Directions: *Make sure you have a watch to time yourself and a No. 2 pencil. When you are ready, start timing yourself, and spend 45 minutes answering the questions in this section. Mark your answers on the Answer Sheet at the end of this section. If you are finished before the time is up, check over your work.*

Language

Directions

Read each of the sentences below. Look at the underlined words in each sentence. There could be an error in punctuation, capitalization, or word usage. If you find an error in a sentence, pick the answer that is the best way to write the underlined words. If there is no error, pick "Correct as is."

Sample

He **must driven** to work every morning.

- ● must drive
- Ⓑ must drove
- Ⓒ must driving
- Ⓓ Correct as is

1 Tom told **principal Marx** about the award.

- Ⓐ Principal marx
- Ⓑ Principal Marx
- Ⓒ principal marx
- Ⓓ Correct as is

2 Gina **said "I saw** my favorite television show last night."

- Ⓕ said, "I saw
- Ⓖ said I see
- Ⓗ says "I saw
- Ⓙ Correct as is

3 Martin **asked, "does** anyone want to go to the movies?"

- Ⓐ asked "Does
- Ⓑ asked "does
- Ⓒ asked, "Does
- Ⓓ Correct as is

4 When you go to the **store, gets** me a newspaper.

- Ⓕ store, get
- Ⓖ Store gets
- Ⓗ store, getting
- Ⓙ Correct as is

5 Markus **said that senator Kraft** will visit our school.

- Ⓐ said, that senator Kraft
- Ⓑ said that Senator Kraft
- Ⓒ said that, senator kraft
- Ⓓ Correct as is

6 Some people like to take a raft on **the Snake river**.

- Ⓕ The snake river
- Ⓖ the snake river
- Ⓗ the Snake River
- Ⓙ Correct as is

GO ON

KAPLAN

7 She <u>types more faster</u> than anyone in the office.

    Ⓐ types more fast

    Ⓑ types fast

    Ⓒ types faster

    Ⓓ Correct as is

8 Domingo dove into the pool and <u>swam to the other end?</u>

    Ⓕ swam to the other end.

    Ⓖ swims to the other end.

    Ⓗ swim to the other end?

    Ⓙ Correct as is

9 The party <u>were</u> fun because of the food and music.

    Ⓐ was

    Ⓑ has

    Ⓒ are

    Ⓓ Correct as is

10 The best principal we ever had <u>was principal Reznor.</u>

    Ⓕ was Principal Reznor

    Ⓖ were Principal reznor

    Ⓗ were principal reznor

    Ⓙ Correct as is

11 Tom <u>and me are going</u> to the game if you will drive us.

    Ⓐ and me are go

    Ⓑ and I are going

    Ⓒ and me were going

    Ⓓ and I is going

GO ON

12 Lisa <u>said that mayor Deriso</u> decided to attend the town meeting.

   (F) have said that mayor Deriso
   (G) said that Mayor Deriso
   (H) say that Mayor Deriso
   (J) Correct as is

13 The principal <u>stated, "everyone</u> should study hard until the end of the year."

   (A) stated, "Everyone
   (B) stated, Everyone
   (C) states, "everyone
   (D) Correct as is

14 When Kiko <u>pushed</u> the curtain back, Roger will walk onto the stage.

   (F) have pushed
   (G) pushes
   (H) are pushing
   (J) Correct as is

15 The car in <u>Mr Fort's</u> parking lot is very nice.

   (A) Mr. Forts
   (B) Mr Forts'
   (C) Mr. Fort's
   (D) Correct as is

16 The team <u>win</u> the game last week.

   (F) will win
   (G) won
   (H) wins
   (J) Correct as is

17 We rode in a raft down <u>the Delaware River</u>.

   (A) The Delaware River
   (B) the Delaware river
   (C) the delaware river
   (D) Correct as is

18 Cleo <u>and me thought</u> about writing the story together.

   (F) and I thought
   (G) and me are thinking
   (H) and I thinks
   (J) Correct as is

GO ON

Directions

Read the words in each of the boxes below. There could be an error in sentence structure. If you find an error in any group of words, pick the answer that is written most clearly and correctly. If there is no error, pick "Correct as is."

Sample

> **Tim went to the store. To buy some groceries.**

- (A) Tim going to the store to buy some groceries.
- ● Tim went to the store to buy some groceries.
- (C) Tim went to the store he buying some groceries.
- (D) Correct as is

19

> **My puppy is finally learning. To walk on a leash.**

- (A) My puppy. She is finally learning to walk on a leash.
- (B) My puppy is finally learning to walking on a leash.
- (C) My puppy is finally learning to walk on a leash.
- (D) Correct as is

20

> **Three birds in the window. They want to come inside.**

- (F) Three birds in the window want to come inside.
- (G) Three birds in the window wanting to come inside.
- (H) Three birds in the window, and they want to come inside.
- (J) Correct as is

21

> **The plane dipped into the clouds, they were dark.**

- (A) The plane dipping into the clouds were dark.
- (B) The plane dipped into the dark clouds.
- (C) The plane dipped into the clouds they were dark.
- (D) Correct as is

22

> **Mrs. Perez opened the door, and she walked outside.**

- (F) Mrs. Perez opened the door. And walking outside she was.
- (G) Mrs. Perez opened the door, she walked outside.
- (H) Mrs. Perez opening the door and walking outside.
- (J) Correct as is

GO ON

23 Wendy did not go to school. Last week.

Ⓐ Wendy did not go. To school last week.

Ⓑ Wendy did not go to school, last week.

Ⓒ Wendy did not go to school last week.

Ⓓ Correct as is

24 Three boys on the field. They wanted to join the game.

Ⓕ Three boys on the field wanted to join the game.

Ⓖ Three boys. On the field wanted to join the game.

Ⓗ Three boys on the field wanting to join the game.

Ⓘ Correct as is

25 The cat was thirsty she drank milk.

Ⓐ The cat was thirsty, and she drank milk.

Ⓑ The cat was thirsty, and she drinking milk.

Ⓒ The cat are thirsty she drank milk.

Ⓓ Correct as is

26 My dog likes to eat peanuts.

Ⓕ My dog likes. To eat peanuts.

Ⓖ My dog liking to eat peanuts.

Ⓗ My dog, likes to eat peanuts.

Ⓘ Correct as is

27 Ms. Tracy plays the piano she gives piano lessons.

Ⓐ Ms. Tracy playing the piano and giving piano lessons.

Ⓑ Ms. Tracy plays the piano and gives piano lessons.

Ⓒ Ms. Tracy plays the piano, gives piano lessons.

Ⓓ Correct as is

28 The bird ate a worm. Then flew away.

Ⓕ The bird ate a worm and then flew away.

Ⓖ The bird ate a worm and then flying away.

Ⓗ The bird ate. A worm then flew away.

Ⓘ Correct as is

GO ON

Directions

Read the paragraph, then answer the questions that follow.

Sample

Dear Aunt Elizabeth,

Thank you for the coins you sent me. How did you know that I needed a 1913 penny to complete my collection? I am so happy.

I hope you will come visit us soon.

Your niece,
Sarah

What is the best topic sentence for this paragraph?

Ⓐ When will you visit?

● Thank you for the coins.

Ⓒ Do you have any nickels?

Ⓓ Coin collecting is fun.

GO ON

Paragraph 1

Dear Cory,

I would like to do some card trading with you. I have three dragon cards and one trainer card. I would like to trade one of my dragon cards for another trainer. Will you trade with me?

Your friend,

Tyler

29 **Which is the best topic sentence for this paragraph?**

ⓐ How are you?

ⓑ The dragons are my favorites.

ⓒ I have a card that I would like to trade with you.

ⓓ Do you have any dragon cards?

30 **Which of these would go best after the last sentence in this paragraph?**

ⓕ I also like basketball cards.

ⓖ Write back and let me know if you want to trade.

ⓗ Do you know how to play games with these cards?

ⓙ How many cards do you have now?

31 **Which of these sentences would not belong in this paragraph?**

ⓐ I want the trainer card because it looks cool.

ⓑ I really do not need three dragon cards.

ⓒ I watched a television show on dragons last night.

ⓓ I also have a wizard card to trade.

GO ON

Paragraph 2

Reading a map is a very important skill. Sometimes you want to know how far away something is. Sometimes you want to know the best way to get somewhere. A map has lots of things that you need to understand. The direction key will show you which way is north. There is also a map key. A map key will show you what different symbols on the map mean.

32 **Which of these would go best after the last sentence?**

- Ⓕ Maps can be big or small.
- Ⓖ If you understand these things, a map will help you get around.
- Ⓗ You can tell a lot about a map by looking at its colors.
- Ⓙ You cannot read a map unless you know about roads.

33 **How could the last two sentences best be combined?**

- Ⓐ There is also a map key that will show you what different symbols on the map mean.
- Ⓑ There is also a map key it will show you what different symbols on the map mean.
- Ⓒ There is also a map key and it will. Show you what different symbols on the map mean.
- Ⓓ There is also a map key will show you what different symbols on the map mean.

34 **Which of these would be the best topic sentence for this paragraph?**

- Ⓕ The direction key has arrows on it to show direction.
- Ⓖ Some maps are harder to read than others.
- Ⓗ Maps have many nice colors on them.
- Ⓙ It is important to be able to read a map and its parts.

35 **Which sentence would not belong in the paragraph?**

- Ⓐ There are old maps and new maps.
- Ⓑ There is more than one reason to use maps.
- Ⓒ Symbols tell you a lot about the map.
- Ⓓ A globe is a helpful way of finding places.

GO ON

Paragraph 3

The class went to the museum on a field trip. The students saw great works of art. Some of the art was very old. Other things in the museum were newer. On the way home, the class voted on its favorite thing at the museum. The students decided that they liked everything that they saw.

36 How could the first two sentences **best** be combined?

- Ⓕ To the museum on a field trip, the class went and the students saw great works of art.
- Ⓖ The class went to the museum on a field trip, and the students saw great works of art.
- Ⓗ Great works of art were seen by the class and went to the museum on a field trip.
- Ⓙ They, the class, saw great works of art and went to the museum on a field trip.

37 Which of these would **not** belong in this paragraph?

- Ⓐ The class also saw old crafts in a section of the museum.
- Ⓑ The students had a wonderful time at the museum.
- Ⓒ The class talked about the art on the way home.
- Ⓓ The zoo is another fun place to visit on class trips.

38 Which of these would be the **best** topic sentence for this paragraph?

- Ⓕ The students voted to find out what everyone liked best.
- Ⓖ The museum is mostly filled with old art, but some of the art is new.
- Ⓗ The students saw many works of art at the museum, and they liked them all.
- Ⓙ The class trip was fun because the students were able to see new things.

Directions

Read each question below. Pick the best answer for each one. Then mark the correct space for the answer that you have picked.

Sample

Look at these guide words from a dictionary page.

> hero — house

Which word could be found on the page?

(A) heart
(B) humid
● high
(D) hurt

39 Look at these guide words from a dictionary page.

> plunge — pocket

Which word could be found on the page?

(A) post
(B) plus
(C) please
(D) pole

40 Look at these guide words from a dictionary page.

> rose — rotate

Which word could be found on the page?

(F) rosin
(G) ruby
(H) rodeo
(J) racer

41 Look at these guide words from a dictionary page.

> ferret — fetch

Which word could be found on the page?

(A) family
(B) fence
(C) fiddle
(D) ferry

42 Which of these is a main heading that includes the other three words?

(F) Hockey
(G) Tennis
(H) Sports
(J) Rugby

43 Which of these is a main heading that includes the other three words?

(A) Horse
(B) Mammal
(C) Monkey
(D) Whale

GO ON

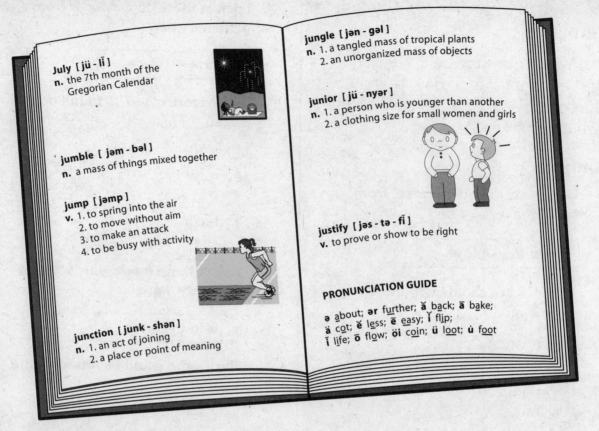

July [jü - lī]
n. the 7th month of the Gregorian Calendar

jumble [jəm - bəl]
n. a mass of things mixed together

jump [jəmp]
v. 1. to spring into the air
2. to move without aim
3. to make an attack
4. to be busy with activity

junction [junk - shən]
n. 1. an act of joining
2. a place or point of meaning

jungle [jən - gəl]
n. 1. a tangled mass of tropical plants
2. an unorganized mass of objects

junior [jü - nyər]
n. 1. a person who is younger than another
2. a clothing size for small women and girls

justify [jəs - tə - fī]
v. to prove or show to be right

PRONUNCIATION GUIDE

ə about; ər further; ă back; ā bake;
ä cot; ĕ less; ē easy; ĭ flip;
ī life; ō flow; öi coin; ü loot; u̇ foot

44 Which definition best fits the word <u>jump</u> as it is used in the sentence below?

My cat likes to <u>jump</u> from the table to the bookshelf.

F 1
G 2
H 3
J 4

45 The first vowel sound in <u>juncture</u> sounds most like the vowel sound in —

A round
B boy
C young
D super

46 What is the correct way to divide <u>justify</u> into syllables?

F just-if-y
G ju-sti-fy
H jus-ti-fy
J just-i-fy

GO ON

47 Look at these guide words from a dictionary page.

| natural — nine |

Which word could be found on the page?

Ⓐ not
Ⓑ noble
Ⓒ nerve
Ⓓ name

48 Which of these is a main heading that includes the other three words?

Ⓕ Rock
Ⓖ Classical
Ⓗ Music
Ⓙ Jazz

STOP

Answer Sheet

1	Ⓐ	Ⓑ	Ⓒ	Ⓓ		25	Ⓐ	Ⓑ	Ⓒ	Ⓓ
2	Ⓕ	Ⓖ	Ⓗ	Ⓙ		26	Ⓕ	Ⓖ	Ⓗ	Ⓙ
3	Ⓐ	Ⓑ	Ⓒ	Ⓓ		27	Ⓐ	Ⓑ	Ⓒ	Ⓓ
4	Ⓕ	Ⓖ	Ⓗ	Ⓙ		28	Ⓕ	Ⓖ	Ⓗ	Ⓙ
5	Ⓐ	Ⓑ	Ⓒ	Ⓓ		29	Ⓐ	Ⓑ	Ⓒ	Ⓓ
6	Ⓕ	Ⓖ	Ⓗ	Ⓙ		30	Ⓕ	Ⓖ	Ⓗ	Ⓙ
7	Ⓐ	Ⓑ	Ⓒ	Ⓓ		31	Ⓐ	Ⓑ	Ⓒ	Ⓓ
8	Ⓕ	Ⓖ	Ⓗ	Ⓙ		32	Ⓕ	Ⓖ	Ⓗ	Ⓙ
9	Ⓐ	Ⓑ	Ⓒ	Ⓓ		33	Ⓐ	Ⓑ	Ⓒ	Ⓓ
10	Ⓕ	Ⓖ	Ⓗ	Ⓙ		34	Ⓕ	Ⓖ	Ⓗ	Ⓙ
11	Ⓐ	Ⓑ	Ⓒ	Ⓓ		35	Ⓐ	Ⓑ	Ⓒ	Ⓓ
12	Ⓕ	Ⓖ	Ⓗ	Ⓙ		36	Ⓕ	Ⓖ	Ⓗ	Ⓙ
13	Ⓐ	Ⓑ	Ⓒ	Ⓓ		37	Ⓐ	Ⓑ	Ⓒ	Ⓓ
14	Ⓕ	Ⓖ	Ⓗ	Ⓙ		38	Ⓕ	Ⓖ	Ⓗ	Ⓙ
15	Ⓐ	Ⓑ	Ⓒ	Ⓓ		39	Ⓐ	Ⓑ	Ⓒ	Ⓓ
16	Ⓕ	Ⓖ	Ⓗ	Ⓙ		40	Ⓕ	Ⓖ	Ⓗ	Ⓙ
17	Ⓐ	Ⓑ	Ⓒ	Ⓢⓗⓔⓔⓣ		41	Ⓐ	Ⓑ	Ⓒ	Ⓓ
18	Ⓕ	Ⓖ	Ⓗ	Ⓙ		42	Ⓕ	Ⓖ	Ⓗ	Ⓙ
19	Ⓐ	Ⓑ	Ⓒ	Ⓓ		43	Ⓐ	Ⓑ	Ⓒ	Ⓓ
20	Ⓕ	Ⓖ	Ⓗ	Ⓙ		44	Ⓕ	Ⓖ	Ⓗ	Ⓙ
21	Ⓐ	Ⓑ	Ⓒ	Ⓓ		45	Ⓐ	Ⓑ	Ⓒ	Ⓓ
22	Ⓕ	Ⓖ	Ⓗ	Ⓙ		46	Ⓕ	Ⓖ	Ⓗ	Ⓙ
23	Ⓐ	Ⓑ	Ⓒ	Ⓓ		47	Ⓐ	Ⓑ	Ⓒ	Ⓓ
24	Ⓕ	Ⓖ	Ⓗ	Ⓙ		48	Ⓕ	Ⓖ	Ⓗ	Ⓙ

Section 6:
Spelling

25 Minutes

30 Questions

Directions: *Make sure you have a watch to time yourself and a No. 2 pencil. When you are ready, start timing yourself, and spend 25 minutes answering the questions in this section. Mark your answers on the Answer Sheet at the end of this section. If you are finished before the time is up, check over your work. This is the last section of the test.*

Spelling

Directions

Read each set of sentences below. Determine whether one of the underlined words in the set is spelled incorrectly or whether there is "No mistake." Then mark the correct space for the answer that you have picked.

Sample

● John is <u>finnishing</u> his homework.
Ⓑ Sarah has <u>gone</u> to the soccer game.
Ⓒ Jim worked on his <u>computer</u> for several hours.
Ⓓ No mistake

1 Ⓐ It was a <u>good</u> rain.
   Ⓑ Where <u>will</u> you go?
   Ⓒ Turn off the <u>ligt</u>.
   Ⓓ No mistake

2 Ⓕ <u>Moisen</u> this towel for me.
   Ⓖ The <u>bird</u> flew away.
   Ⓗ <u>Here</u> we are.
   Ⓙ No mistake

3 Ⓐ Joan <u>looked</u> happy.
   Ⓑ My <u>jacket</u> is warm.
   Ⓒ The <u>hors</u> jumped the fence.
   Ⓓ No mistake

4 Ⓕ I feel <u>full</u>.
   Ⓖ The <u>brook</u> has no water.
   Ⓗ Put your <u>toys</u> away.
   Ⓙ No mistake

5 Ⓐ I will arrive <u>Thursday</u>.
   Ⓑ Close the <u>curtanes</u> at night.
   Ⓒ The play was <u>rather</u> long.
   Ⓓ No mistake

6 Ⓕ Susan <u>rushed</u> home for lunch.
   Ⓖ The <u>messige</u> was lost.
   Ⓗ That is my <u>own</u> dog.
   Ⓙ No mistake

GO ON

7 Ⓐ The belt <u>buckel</u> was broken.
   Ⓑ The pool <u>needs</u> more water.
   Ⓒ Can you <u>forgive</u> me?
   Ⓓ No mistake

8 Ⓕ <u>Place</u> it in the closet.
   Ⓖ I am very <u>grateful</u>.
   Ⓗ The <u>wether</u> was nice.
   Ⓙ No mistake

9 Ⓐ We traveled for one <u>week</u>.
   Ⓑ <u>Would</u> you like to go?
   Ⓒ The shell was very <u>tuff</u>.
   Ⓓ No mistake

10 Ⓕ The <u>wind</u> was fierce.
   Ⓖ Let's go to the <u>beech</u>.
   Ⓗ Hold onto your <u>tickets</u>.
   Ⓙ No mistake

11 Ⓐ The <u>knife</u> was sharp.
   Ⓑ Who <u>cauzed</u> this to happen?
   Ⓒ You play the <u>piano</u> well.
   Ⓓ No mistake

12 Ⓕ Our dog <u>eats</u> a lot of food.
   Ⓖ Take this <u>pill</u> for your cold.
   Ⓗ The jacket <u>butten</u> popped off.
   Ⓙ No mistake

13 Ⓐ Have you <u>thought</u> it over.
   Ⓑ He <u>would</u> not leave.
   Ⓒ The fence was painted <u>wite</u>.
   Ⓓ No mistake

GO ON

14
F The speech was <u>brief</u>.
G <u>Please</u> be careful.
H I <u>hope</u> you enjoyed your stay.
J No mistake

15
A It was hard to <u>controle</u> the car.
B The <u>board</u> member spoke.
C She tripped <u>carelessly</u> on the ice.
D No mistake

16
F Jake <u>stacked</u> the blocks.
G These <u>shoes</u> are in fashion.
H The <u>erlier</u> version was better.
J No mistake

17
A The <u>chek</u> did not arrive.
B Joseph is our best <u>player</u>.
C The <u>rooster</u> woke up.
D No mistake

18
F My <u>mittens</u> are blue.
G <u>Somthing</u> is wrong.
H Take a <u>number</u>.
J No Mistake

19
A We <u>wanted</u> to continue.
B I <u>regret</u> my actions.
C Is <u>anybody</u> home?
D No mistake

20
F The <u>decision</u> is final.
G Let's <u>gril</u> some burgers.
H They have <u>nothing</u>.
J No mistake

21
A Take that cat <u>home</u>.
B It was a narrow <u>ledge</u>.
C He was an <u>honest</u> man.
D No mistake

GO ON

22
- Ⓕ This is <u>truley</u> good.
- Ⓖ The <u>dessert</u> was chocolate pie.
- Ⓗ I will <u>field</u> that question.
- Ⓙ No mistake

23
- Ⓐ Jack kept the door <u>prize</u>.
- Ⓑ He has an <u>orange</u> shirt.
- Ⓒ Our <u>visits</u> were fun.
- Ⓓ No mistake

24
- Ⓕ I drew a <u>rainbow</u>.
- Ⓖ What a <u>griping</u> story!
- Ⓗ Mark is a <u>golfer</u>.
- Ⓙ No mistake

25
- Ⓐ The soup is <u>boiling</u>.
- Ⓑ He is <u>unnlike</u> everyone else.
- Ⓒ We walked through the <u>park</u>.
- Ⓓ No mistake

26
- Ⓕ The <u>tools</u> are in the shed.
- Ⓖ Dan <u>cryed</u> during the movie.
- Ⓗ <u>About</u> then people showed up.
- Ⓙ No mistake

27
- Ⓐ Use a number 2 <u>pensil</u>.
- Ⓑ I <u>bought</u> carrots.
- Ⓒ The <u>events</u> are at the same time.
- Ⓓ No mistake

28
- Ⓕ <u>Sadley</u>, I cannot make it.
- Ⓖ Take the blue <u>marker</u>.
- Ⓗ The paint is still <u>drying</u>.
- Ⓙ No mistake

29
- Ⓐ There are no <u>monkeys</u> here.
- Ⓑ Have a graham <u>cracker</u>.
- Ⓒ It is a <u>generus</u> offer.
- Ⓓ No mistake

30
- Ⓕ These <u>coupons</u> have expired.
- Ⓖ You are <u>makeing</u> a mess.
- Ⓗ The tea was <u>terribly</u> hot.
- Ⓙ No mistake

STOP

Answer Sheet

1 Ⓐ Ⓑ Ⓒ Ⓓ   16 Ⓕ Ⓖ Ⓗ Ⓙ
2 Ⓕ Ⓖ Ⓗ Ⓙ   17 Ⓐ Ⓑ Ⓒ Ⓓ
3 Ⓐ Ⓑ Ⓒ Ⓓ   18 Ⓕ Ⓖ Ⓗ Ⓙ
4 Ⓕ Ⓖ Ⓗ Ⓙ   19 Ⓐ Ⓑ Ⓒ Ⓓ
5 Ⓐ Ⓑ Ⓒ Ⓓ   20 Ⓕ Ⓖ Ⓗ Ⓙ
6 Ⓕ Ⓖ Ⓗ Ⓙ   21 Ⓐ Ⓑ Ⓒ Ⓓ
7 Ⓐ Ⓑ Ⓒ Ⓓ   22 Ⓕ Ⓖ Ⓗ Ⓙ
8 Ⓕ Ⓖ Ⓗ Ⓙ   23 Ⓐ Ⓑ Ⓒ Ⓓ
9 Ⓐ Ⓑ Ⓒ Ⓓ   24 Ⓕ Ⓖ Ⓗ Ⓙ
10 Ⓕ Ⓖ Ⓗ Ⓙ   25 Ⓐ Ⓑ Ⓒ Ⓓ
11 Ⓐ Ⓑ Ⓒ Ⓓ   26 Ⓕ Ⓖ Ⓗ Ⓙ
12 Ⓕ Ⓖ Ⓗ Ⓙ   27 Ⓐ Ⓑ Ⓒ Ⓓ
13 Ⓐ Ⓑ Ⓒ Ⓓ   28 Ⓕ Ⓖ Ⓗ Ⓙ
14 Ⓕ Ⓖ Ⓗ Ⓙ   29 Ⓐ Ⓑ Ⓒ Ⓓ
15 Ⓐ Ⓑ Ⓒ Ⓓ   30 Ⓕ Ⓖ Ⓗ Ⓙ

PRACTICE TEST *B*

Answer Key

Reading Vocabulary

1 D
2 G
3 A
4 H
5 C
6 H
7 C
8 G
9 A
10 J
11 A
12 J
13 C
14 G
15 D
16 F
17 D
18 F
19 C
20 J
21 D
22 H
23 B
24 J
25 A
26 F
27 D
28 G
29 C
30 F

Reading Comprehension

1 C
2 G
3 C
4 F
5 B
6 H
7 A
8 H
9 C
10 F
11 B
12 F
13 A
14 G
15 B
16 G
17 B
18 J
19 B
20 J
21 A
22 J
23 C
24 F
25 B
26 F
27 D
28 H
29 A
30 J
31 B
32 H
33 C
34 F
35 B
36 H
37 A
38 G
39 D
40 F
41 D
42 F
43 C
44 F
45 D
46 G
47 C
48 H
49 D
50 F
51 B
52 F
53 D
54 J

Mathematics—Problem Solving

1	B	24	G
2	H	25	B
3	B	26	G
4	H	27	B
5	B	28	F
6	G	29	C
7	A	30	H
8	F	31	A
9	B	32	J
10	F	33	A
11	B	34	H
12	G	35	B
13	C	36	G
14	G	37	B
15	B	38	J
16	J	39	A
17	B	40	H
18	F	41	B
19	D	42	H
20	J	43	A
21	C	44	G
22	H	45	C
23	B	46	J

Mathematics—Procedures

1	C
2	H
3	A
4	G
5	A
6	H
7	C
8	G
9	B
10	F
11	C
12	H
13	A
14	F
15	B
16	K
17	B
18	K
19	D
20	G
21	C
22	G
23	C
24	J
25	B
26	H
27	B
28	J
29	A
30	G

Language

1	B	25	A
2	F	26	J
3	C	27	B
4	F	28	F
5	B	29	C
6	H	30	G
7	C	31	C
8	F	32	G
9	A	33	A
10	F	34	J
11	B	35	D
12	G	36	G
13	A	37	D
14	G	38	H
15	C	39	B
16	G	40	F
17	D	41	D
18	F	42	H
19	C	43	B
20	F	44	F
21	B	45	C
22	J	46	H
23	C	47	C
24	F	48	H

Spelling

1	C
2	F
3	C
4	J
5	B
6	G
7	A
8	H
9	C
10	G
11	B
12	H
13	C
14	J
15	A
16	H
17	A
18	G
19	D
20	G
21	D
22	F
23	D
24	G
25	B
26	G
27	A
28	F
29	C
30	G

How Did We Do? Grade Us.

Thank you for choosing a Kaplan book. Your comments and suggestions are very useful to us. Please answer the following questions to assist us in our continued development of high-quality resources to meet your needs.

The title of the Kaplan book I read was: _____

My name is: _____

My address is: _____

_____

My e-mail address is: _____

What overall grade would you give this book? ⓐ ⓑ ⓒ ⓓ Ⓕ

How relevant was the information to your goals? ⓐ ⓑ ⓒ ⓓ Ⓕ

How comprehensive was the information in this book? ⓐ ⓑ ⓒ ⓓ Ⓕ

How accurate was the information in this book? ⓐ ⓑ ⓒ ⓓ Ⓕ

How easy was the book to use? ⓐ ⓑ ⓒ ⓓ Ⓕ

How appealing was the book's design? ⓐ ⓑ ⓒ ⓓ Ⓕ

What were the book's strong points? _____

How could this book be improved? _____

Is there anything that we left out that you wanted to know more about?

Would you recommend this book to others? ☐ YES   ☐ NO

Other comments: _____

_____

_____

Do we have permission to quote you? ☐ YES   ☐ NO

Thank you for your help.
Please tear out this page and mail it to:

Managing Editor
Kaplan, Inc.
888 Seventh Avenue
New York, NY 10106

KAPLAN®

Thanks!

©1999 SCORE! Educational Centers

You can always tell when there's a SCORE! Educational Center in the neighborhood.

Kids who discover *SCORE!* move a little faster than typical students. In fact, students typically make a full year of progress in just 5 months at *SCORE!*. We foster a love of learning by nurturing children in an upbeat, positive environment. Our afterschool and weekend drop-in sessions provide children in grades K–10 with personalized learning programs to help them successfully meet their individual goals. Come discover just how fast your child can be.

To learn more about how SCORE! can help your child meet his or her learning goals, call 1-800-49SCORE or visit us at www.escore.com today!

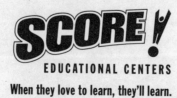

SCORE!
EDUCATIONAL CENTERS

When they love to learn, they'll learn.